2nd EDITION

Pupil Book 3C

Series Editor: Peter Clarke

Authors: Elizabeth Jurgensen, Jeanette Mumford, Sandra Roberts

Contents

Unit 9	Page number
Week 1: Number – Number and place value	
Lesson 1: Raffle tickets	4
Lesson 2: Number lines	5
Lesson 3: Partitioning 3-digit numbers	6
Lesson 4: What's my number?	7
Week 2: Number – Addition and subtraction	
Lesson 1: Adding and subtracting mentally	8
Lesson 2: Column addition (3)	9
Lesson 3: Column subtraction (3)	10
Lesson 4: Fowl problems	11
Week 3: Geometry – Properties of shape	
Lesson 1: Horizontal and vertical lines	12
Lesson 2: Perpendicular and parallel lines	13
Lesson 3: Pick and choose shapes	14
Lesson 4: More about 3-D shapes	15

Unit 10	
Week 1: Number – Multiplication and division	
Lesson 1: Multiplication using partitioning	16
Lesson 2: Multiplication using partitioning and the grid method	17
Lesson 3: Multiplication: Introducing the expanded written method	18
Lesson 4: Solving word problems (7)	19
Week 2: Number – Fractions	
Lesson 1: Investigate fractions	20
Lesson 2: Fraction problems	21
Lesson 3: Equivalent fraction puzzle	22
Lesson 4: Tenths	23
Week 3: Measurement (volume and capacity)	
Lesson 1: Fractions of 1 litre	24
Lesson 2: Millilitres more or less	25
Lesson 3: Shopping litres	26
Lesson 4: Adding and subtracting capacities	27

Unit 11

Page number

Week 1: **Number – Addition and subtraction, incl. Measurement (money)**

Lesson 1:	Estimating and checking column addition	28
Lesson 2:	Addition target answers	29
Lesson 3:	Adding and subtracting money	30
Lesson 4:	School shopping	31

Week 2: **Number – Addition and subtraction**

Lesson 1:	Estimating and checking column subtraction	32
Lesson 2:	Subtraction target answers	33
Lesson 3:	Jumping forward to the target	34
Lesson 4:	Jumping back to the target	35

Week 3: **Measurement (time)**

Lesson 1:	Just a minute	36
Lesson 2:	Race times	37
Lesson 3:	Using a calendar	38
Lesson 4:	Cycle race times	39

Unit 12

Week 1: **Number – Multiplication and division**

Lesson 1:	Multiplication using the expanded written method	40
Lesson 2:	Multiplication: Introducing the formal written method (1)	41
Lesson 3:	Multiplication: Introducing the formal written method (2)	42
Lesson 4:	Solving word problems (8)	43

Week 2: **Number – Multiplication and division**

Lesson 1:	Division using partitioning	44
Lesson 2:	Division using the expanded written method	45
Lesson 3:	Division using the formal written method	46
Lesson 4:	Solving word problems (9)	47

Week 3: **Statistics**

Lesson 1:	School disco pictograms	48
Lesson 2:	Activities bar charts	50
Lesson 3:	On the menu pictograms	52
Lesson 4:	Off to Italy bar charts	54

Maths facts 56

Raffle tickets

Compare and order numbers up to 1,000

Challenge 1

1 What two raffle ticket numbers come after these tickets?

2 What raffle ticket numbers come before and after these tickets?

Challenge 2

1 What three raffle ticket numbers come after these tickets?

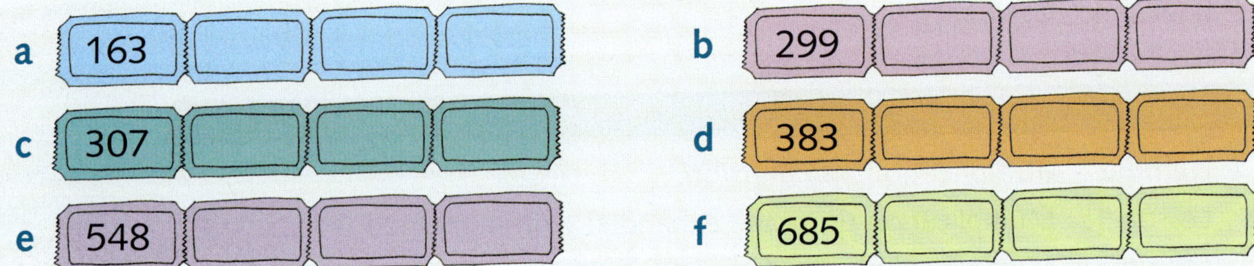

2 What raffle ticket numbers come before and after these tickets?

3 These winning numbers are read out. Write the number in numerals.

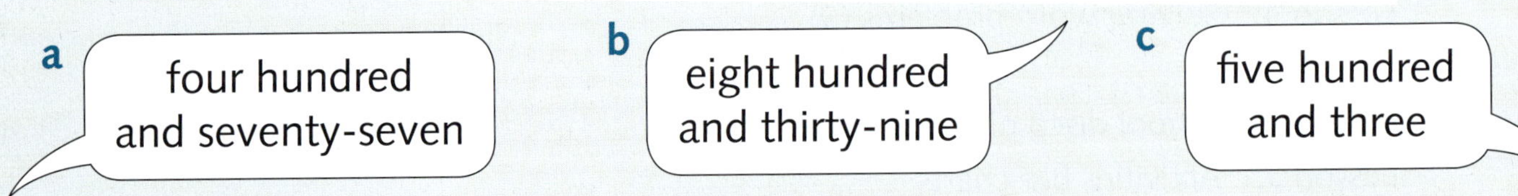

Challenge 3

What three raffle ticket numbers come before these tickets?

Number lines

Order numbers to 1,000 on an empty number line

You will need:
- Resource 43: Number lines

1 Use the 0–100 number line. Put these numbers on the number line.

2 Use the 100–200 number line. Put these numbers on the number line.

llenge 2

1 Use the 0–200 number line.

a Put these numbers on the number line.

b Now write in another number between each of the numbers.

2 Use the 0–500 number line.

a Put these numbers on the number line.

b Now write in another number between each of the numbers.

1 Use the 500–1,000 number line.

a Put these numbers on the number line.

b Now write in another number between each of the numbers.

2 This book of raffle tickets contains odd numbers only.
Which three raffle ticket numbers come after these tickets?

a 

b 

c 

d 

e 

f 919

Partitioning 3-digit numbers

Decompose 3-digit numbers in different ways

You will need:
- Base 10

Challenge 1

Decompose these numbers into 100s, 10s and 1s using Base 10.

a 128 **b** 152
c 177 **d** 216
e 258 **f** 341
g 309 **h** 458
i 473 **j** 514

Example

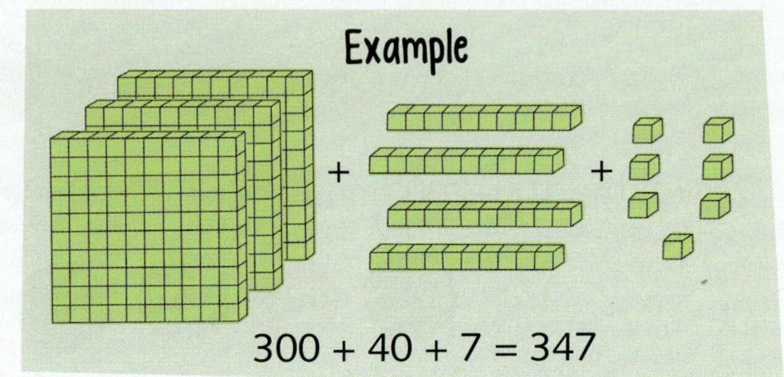

300 + 40 + 7 = 347

Challenge 2

1 Regroup these numbers in as many different ways as you can. Only decompose the 100s. If you need to, use the Base 10 to help you.

a 356 **b** 372 **c** 484 **d** 447
e 563 **f** 592 **g** 642 **h** 684

Example

461
400 + 60 + 1
300 + 160 + 1
200 + 260 + 1
100 + 360 + 1

2 Using the same numbers as in Question 1, regroup each number in four different ways. This time only decompose the 10s.

Example

461
400 + 60 + 1
400 + 50 + 11
400 + 40 + 21
400 + 30 + 31

Challenge 3

Find the missing numbers.

a ☐ + 120 + 6 = 526
b ☐ + 350 + 9 = 759
c ☐ + 460 + 15 = 875
d 200 + ☐ + 13 = 463
e 300 + ☐ + 63 = 793
f ☐ + 260 + ☐ = 587
g 300 + ☐ + ☐ = 762
h 500 + ☐ + ☐ = 947

What's my number?

Solve number problems and reason mathematically

What's my number?

Write down some questions that you will ask your partner about their secret number.

Take turns to:

- ask your partner the questions and use the number square to cross out numbers that are *not* their secret number
- guess your partner's secret number.

Use these words and phrases to help you write questions and list the properties:
odd
even
multiple of 10 / 5 / 3
more than
less than
between
place value
digit
hundreds / tens / ones

enge

1 Secretly write down a number from the 101–200 number square. List all the properties of the number that you know.

2 Play 'What's my number?' with a partner.

You will need:

- Resource 44: 101–200 number square

enge

1 Secretly write down a number from the 201–500 number square. List all the properties of the number that you know.

2 Play 'What's my number?' with a partner.

You will need:

- Resource 45: 201–500 number square

enge

1 Secretly write down a number between 101 and 1,000. List all the properties of the number that you know.

2 Play 'What's my number?' with a partner.

Adding and subtracting mentally

Add and subtract numbers mentally

Challenge 1

1 Work out these addition calculations. Show any working out.

a 45 + 36 b 52 + 27 c 48 + 50 d 74 + 60

e 146 + 7 f 183 + 9 g 137 + 200 h 243 + 400

2 Work out these subtraction calculations. Show any working out.

a 94 – 37 b 68 – 25 c 137 – 40 d 186 – 70

e 231 – 7 f 275 – 6 g 461 – 200 h 576 – 300

Challenge 2

1 Work out these addition and subtraction calculations.

a 356 + 80 = □ b 276 + 500 = ○ c 421 – 70 = △

d 386 + 9 = △ e 721 – 400 = □ f □ = 402 – 7

g ○ = 78 + 84 h △ = 91 – 53 i ○ = 573 + 60

2 Work out these missing number calculations.

a 356 + △ = 396 b 257 + □ = 264 c 382 – ○ = 302

d 541 – ○ = 141 e 445 = 385 + □ f 516 = 595 – △

g 84 = 35 + ○ h 72 = 97 – △ i 465 + □ = 515

Challenge 3

Work out these missing number calculations.

a 673 + □ = 743 b 704 – ○ = 697 c 989 – 689 = □

d 641 – △ = 551 e 792 = 292 + □ f 843 = 753 + △

g △ – 70 = 361 h ○ + 50 = 486 i 80 + ○ = 863

Column addition (3)

- Add 3-digit numbers using the formal written method of column addition
- Estimate and check the answer to the calculation

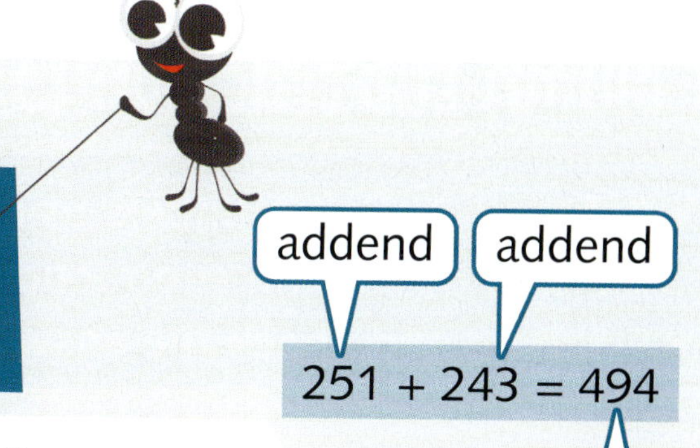

Write four different addition calculations for each question using the numbers given as the addends. First estimate the answer to each calculation. Then use the formal method to work out the answer.

1 132 310 251 326 243

2 237 145 329 258 316

1 436 357 419 238 547

2 563 494 265 471 382

1 327 292 581 463 418

2 365 475 486 494 387

Column subtraction (3)

- Subtract 3-digit numbers using the formal written method of column subtraction
- Estimate and check the answer to the calculation

Write different subtraction calculations for each question.

- Choose a number from the green box for the minuend.
- Choose a number from the blue box for the subtrahend.
- First estimate the answers to your calculations. Then work them out using the formal written method.

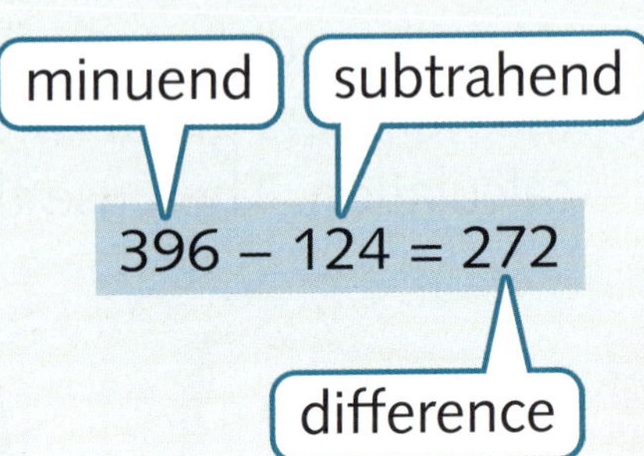

Challenge 1 Write four calculations for each question.

1 | 367, 396, 378, 389 | – | 235, 124, 264, 151

2 | 384, 375, 363, 392 | – | 216, 247, 258, 236

Challenge 2 Write four calculations for each question.

1 | 463, 472, 581, 594 | – | 247, 329, 358, 236

2 | 418, 427, 546, 535 | – | 362, 274, 391, 183

Challenge 3 Write eight calculations.

628, 749, 682, 817, 926, 783, 891, 983 – 473, 382, 518, 539, 327, 282, 493, 328

Fowl problems

Solve problems and reason mathematically

Work out these word problems. Show your working out.

1 The chickens laid 67 eggs on Monday and 56 eggs on Tuesday. How many eggs were laid in those two days?

2 In one week 145 eggs were laid. The following week 80 eggs were laid. How many eggs were laid in those two weeks?

3 The chickens ate 246 g of food one week and 253 g the next week. How much food was eaten in those two weeks?

4 In one term the total number of eggs laid was 472. The cook used 300. How many eggs were left to sell?

1 The school cook needs 73 eggs today. However, the chickens have only laid 47. How many more eggs does she need?

2 The school collected 30 eggs this morning. They put them in boxes of 6 ready to sell. How many boxes do they have?

3 The chicken food costs the school £365 for a year. The eggs sell for £648 that year. How much money does the school make?

4 There were 342 eggs. The cook took 70. How many eggs were left?

1 The local restaurant orders 24 eggs daily. How many will it buy in a week?

2 The school target is 675 eggs this half term. So far they have collected 400. How many more eggs do they need to reach their target?

3 Next term the school wants to buy 50 more chickens. Then they will have 268 altogether. How many chickens do they have now?

4 In the Autumn term 575 eggs were collected before half term and 347 after half term. How many eggs were collected altogether?

Horizontal and vertical lines

Know when a line is horizontal or vertical

Challenge 1

Look at the red line on each object. Write H if it is horizontal and V if it is vertical.

Challenge 2

Copy these shapes on to 1 cm squared paper. Draw the horizontal lines in blue. Draw the vertical lines in red.

You will need:
- 1 cm squared paper
- ruler
- blue and red pencils

Challenge 3

Copy and continue the pattern. Draw horizontal lines in blue, vertical lines in red and diagonal lines in green.

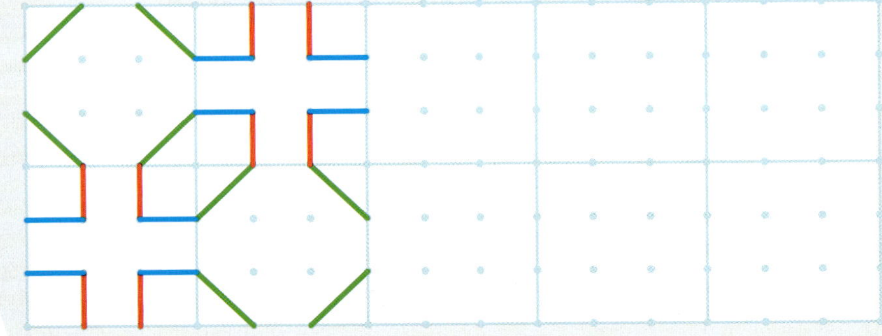

You will need:
- 1 cm squared dot paper
- ruler
- blue, red and green pencils

Perpendicular and parallel lines

Recognise perpendicular and parallel lines

llenge 1

The corners of the football pitch are marked A, B, C and D.

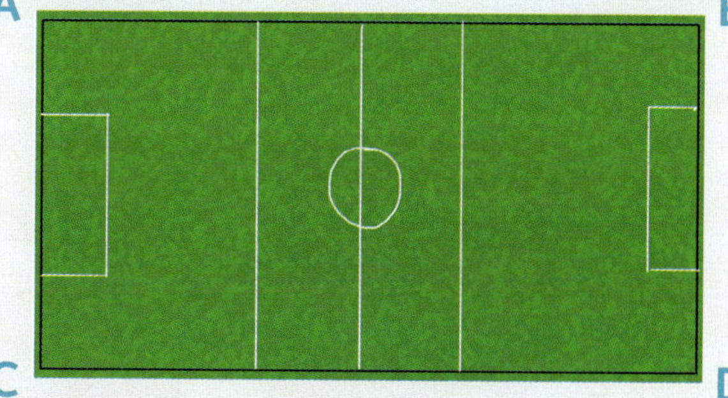

a Which side is parallel to side AB?

b Which side is perpendicular to side DC?

llenge 2

This is Helen's house.

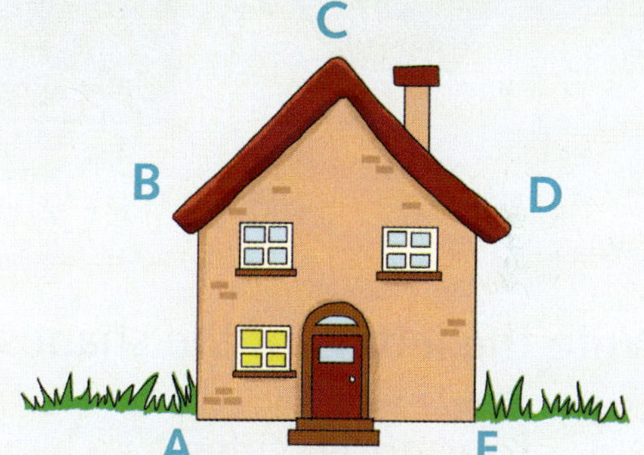

1 a Name two pairs of perpendicular lines.

b Name one pair of parallel lines.

2 a Draw the shapes below on squared paper.

b Mark all the perpendicular and parallel lines.

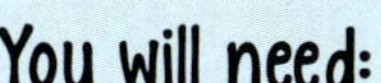

You will need:
- 1 cm squared paper
- ruler

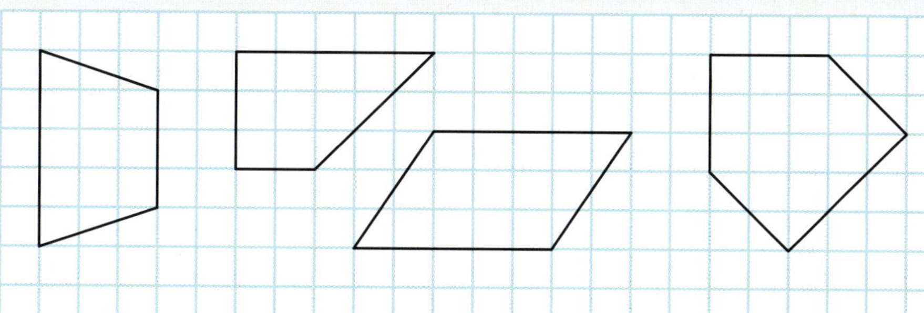

Example

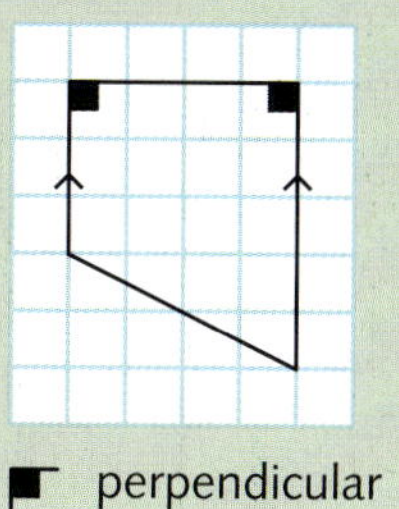

perpendicular

parallel

enge 3

The cube is on a horizontal table.
Look at the face labelled A, B, C and D.
Name two pairs of edges which are:

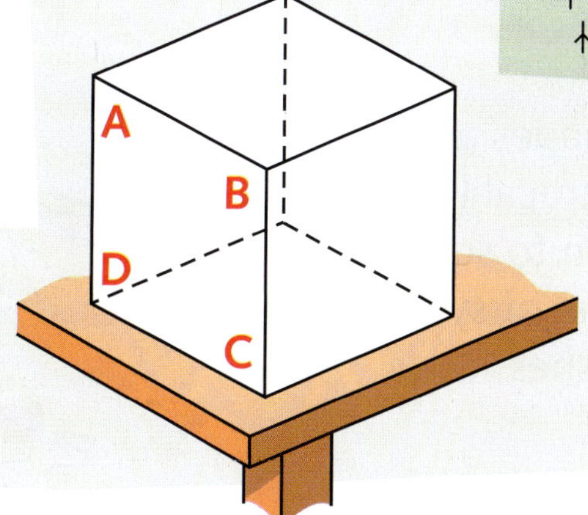

a perpendicular to the table top

b parallel to the table top

Pick and choose shapes

Describe the properties of 2-D shapes

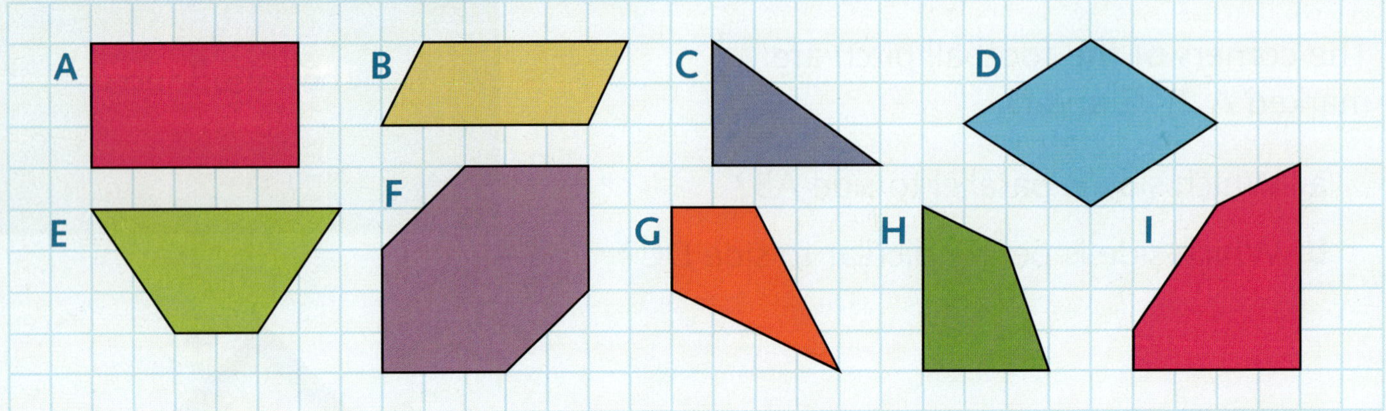

Challenge 1

Write the letters of the shapes above that have:

- **a** four equal sides
- **b** two pairs of equal sides
- **c** at least one right angle
- **d** one pair of parallel sides

Challenge 2

Write the letters of the shapes above that have:

- **a** four sides and one right angle
- **b** two pairs of parallel sides
- **c** four vertices and opposite sides equal
- **d** all sides a different length
- **e** two pairs of perpendicular sides
- **f** two angles greater than a right angle and four equal sides

Challenge 3

Copy the shapes above that have one vertical line of symmetry on to squared paper. Mark the line of symmetry with red dashes.

You will need:
- 1 cm squared paper
- ruler
- red pencil

More about 3-D shapes

Describe the properties of 3-D shapes

allenges ,2,3

These 3-D shapes are made with straws.

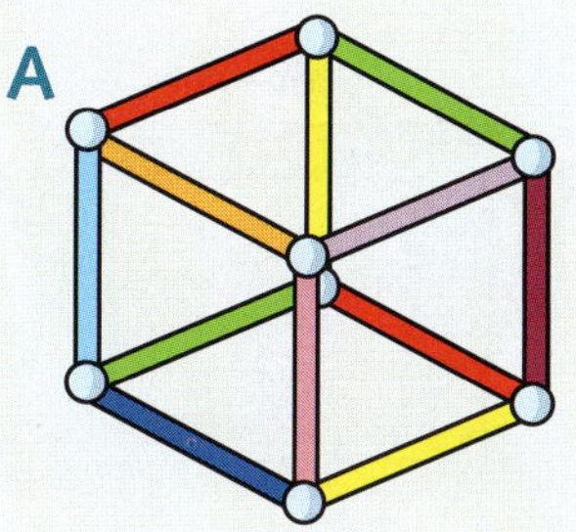

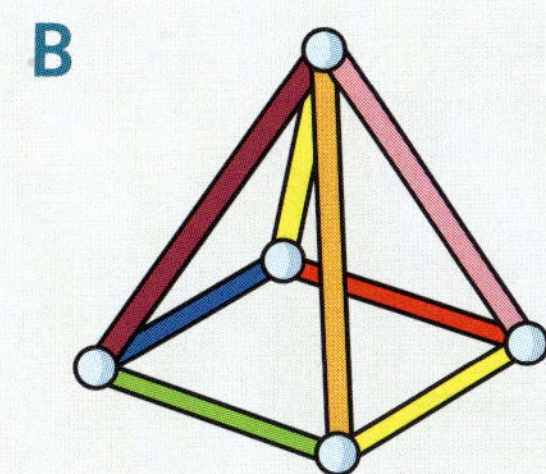

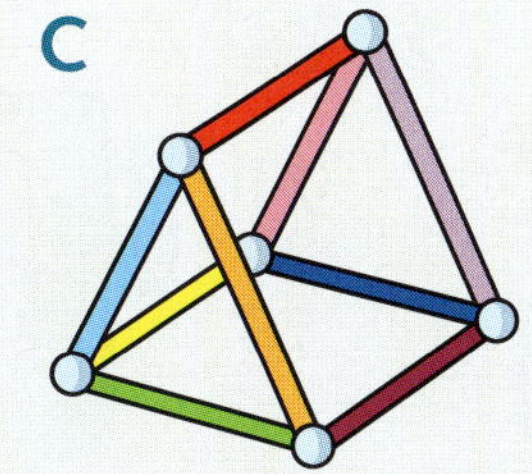

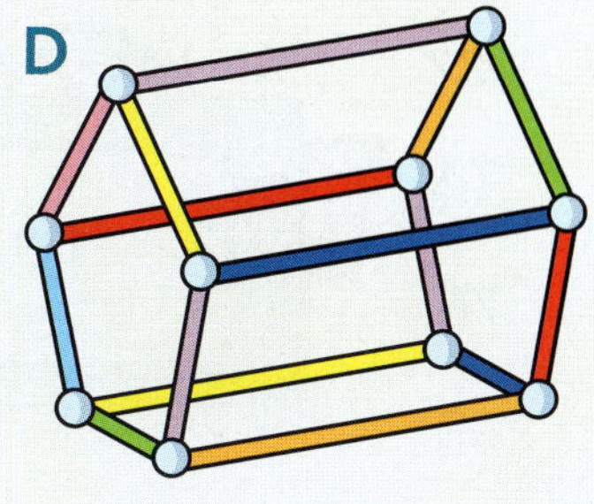

Write which shapes have:

a three edges only at each vertex

b triangular and square faces

c more than one right-angled face

d angles greater than a right angle

allenges 2,3

A cuboid and a triangular prism are on a horizontal table.
Write which 3-D shape has:

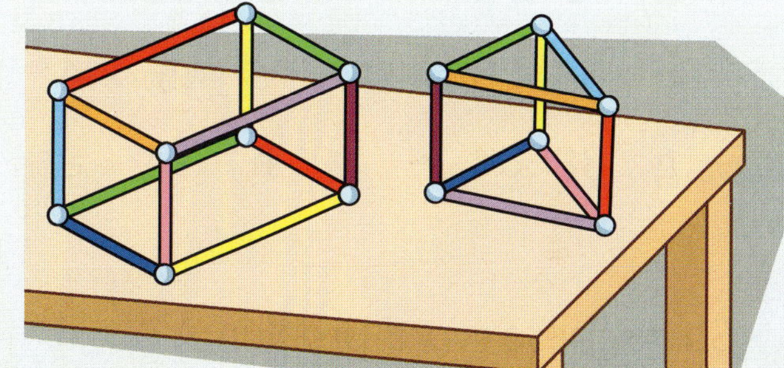

a three vertical faces

b four vertical faces

c eight horizontal edges

d six horizontal edges

allenge 3

Ethan built these skeletal cubes with interlocking cubes. Copy and complete the table.

Skeletal cube	Number of horizontal cubes	Number of vertical cubes	Total
3 by 3 by 3			
4 by 4 by 4			
5 by 5 by 5			

Multiplication using partitioning

Use partitioning to calculate TO × O

Example
32 = 30 + 2

Challenge 1

Partition these numbers into 10s and 1s.

1. 25, 34, 76, 43 — Tens | Ones
2. 68, 71, 16, 46 — Tens | Ones
3. 54, 87, 39, 23 — Tens | Ones

Challenge 2

Estimate the answer first, then partition each of these calculations to work out the answer.

Example
63 × 5 → 60 × 5 = 300
= (60 × 5) + (3 × 5)
= 300 + 15
= 315

a	47 × 5	b	32 × 4	c	64 × 3
d	53 × 5	e	26 × 4	f	74 × 3
g	38 × 4	h	91 × 8	i	85 × 3

Challenge 3

Solve these word problems.

1. Martin receives 27 birthday cards every year for his birthday. He is now 8 years old. How many cards has he received in total?
2. Candles are sold in packs of 39. How many candles in 4 packs?
3. Wrapping paper is sold in 3 metre rolls. Jamie buys 48 rolls. How many metres of wrapping paper in total?
4. A birthday cake needs to be ordered 2 weeks in advance. Martin's birthday is on the 25th May. What is the last date on which the cake can be ordered?

Multiplication using partitioning and the grid method

Use the grid method to calculate TO × O

Example

63 × 8 → 60 × 8 = 480

Challenge 1

Estimate the answer to each calculation.

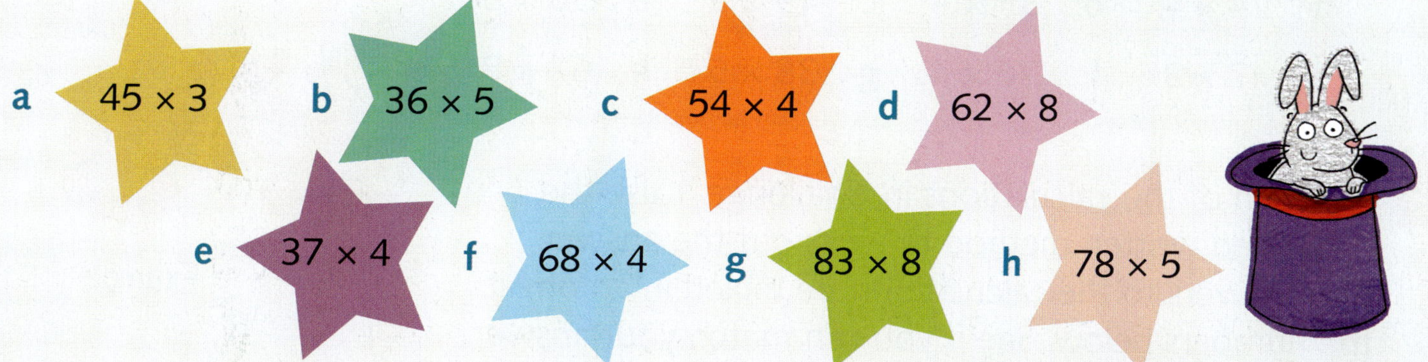

Challenge 2

Use the grid method to work out the answers to the calculations in Challenge 1. Match the answers to your calculations to one of these answers to see if you are correct.

Example

63 × 8

×	60	3	
8	480	24	= 504

272 496 390 216 664 180 148 135

Challenge 3

Play this game with a partner.

- Each player takes turns to choose a number from the cards below and to spin the spinner.
- Estimate first, then multiply your two numbers. Show your working out.
- The person with the largest answer scores one point.
- Choose a different number card each time.
- The first person to score five points is the winner.

You will need:

- Resource 36: 2, 3, 4, 5, 8 and 10 spinner

65 38 42 27 39 56 84 16 72 83 78

Multiplication: Introducing the expanded written method

Use the expanded written method to calculate TO × O

Challenge 1

Estimate the answer to each calculation.

Example

63 × 8 → 60 × 8 = 480

a	24 × 4	**b**	33 × 4	**c**	49 × 3	**d**	56 × 8
e	47 × 3	**f**	76 × 4	**g**	38 × 5	**h**	67 × 8

Challenge 2

For each of the calculations in Challenge 1 use the expanded written method to work out the answer. The answers to the calculations are mixed in amongst the numbers below. See if you can match your answer with one of the answers below.

Example

		6	3	
×			8	
		2	4	(3 × 8)
	4	8	0	(60 × 8)
	5	0	4	
	1			

Challenge 3

Three of the flowers below do not belong.
Find the odd ones out and explain how they are different.

44 × 4

88 × 2

78 × 2

36 × 3

54 × 5

22 × 8

27 × 4

54 × 2

53 × 4

Solving word problems (7)

Solve word problems and reason mathematically

1 a $7 \times 3 =$ b $70 \times 3 =$	**2** a $3 \times 8 =$ b $30 \times 8 =$	**3** a $6 \times 4 =$ b $60 \times 4 =$	**4** a $9 \times 3 =$ b $90 \times 3 =$
5 a $7 \times 5 =$ b $70 \times 5 =$	**6** a $6 \times 8 =$ b $60 \times 8 =$	**7** a $7 \times 4 =$ b $70 \times 4 =$	**8** a $9 \times 2 =$ b $90 \times 2 =$

llenge 2

Choose a container of items from the pictures below. Spin the spinner and write a multiplication calculation. First estimate and then work out the answer.

You will need:

- Resource 36: 2, 3, 4, 5, 8 and 10 spinner

lenge 3

Use the pictures above to answer these questions.

1. If you have 3 boxes of scissors, how many scissors do you have?
2. How many coloured pencils are there in 3 pots?
3. How many glue sticks are there in 8 boxes?
4. The class had 100 paintbrushes but some are now missing. How many are missing?
5. Year 3 need 100 coloured pencils. They have 1 pot. How many more pencils do they need?
6. The school orders 10 boxes of glue sticks in Term 1, 5 boxes in Term 2 and 8 boxes in Term 3. How many glue sticks are ordered in total for the year?
7. The school has run out of scissors. They order 1 box. If each pair of scissors costs £2, how much does the box cost?
8. There are 320 children in Key Stage 2. If the school buys 3 pots of felt tips, will there be enough for every child? How many more are needed or how many extra are there?

Investigate fractions

Find fractions of amounts

You will need:
- 15 counters

Challenge 1

1 How many fractions can you divide 12 counters into? Try out different fractions to see if they work.

Record it like this: **12**

$\frac{1}{2}$ of 12 is

2 Now try with 15 counters.

You will need:
- 20 counters

Challenge 2

1 How many fractions can you divide 16 counters into? Try out different fractions to see if they work. Record the fractions that divide equally and the fractions that do not divide equally.

Record it like this: **16**

$\frac{1}{2}$ of 16 = 16 ÷ 2 =

$\frac{1}{3}$ of 16 = 16 ÷ 3 Does not divide equally

2 Now try with 20 counters.

3 Choose your own number to investigate.

Challenge 3

1 How many fractions can you divide 24 into equally? Use division to find the fractions.

Record it like this: **24**

$\frac{1}{2}$ of 24 = 24 ÷ 2 =

2 Now investigate 30.

3 Explain the link between fractions and multiplication and division.

Fraction problems

Solve fraction word problems and reason mathematically

1 Louis gets £6 pocket money every week. He always spends half on a comic. How much does the comic cost?

2 Poppy the cat sleeps for 8 hours every day. She spends half of her sleeping time on the bed and half in the garden. For how many hours does she sleep on the bed?

3 It takes Granny 12 minutes to walk to the shop. Half way she rests on a bench. How long does it take her to walk to the bench?

4 John chooses 20 grams of sweets at the pick and mix. Mum says he can eat half before tea. How many grams are left?

1 Kalshuma has £12 to spend. She buys a bag that costs a quarter of her money. How much does she have left?

2 Ben is allowed to watch 60 minutes of TV every day. His favourite programme takes a third of his time. How long does he have left?

3 Ella's dog weighs 8 kg. The vet says he needs to go on a diet and lose a quarter of his weight. How much does he need to lose?

4 The maths lesson was 60 minutes long. The class spent a quarter of the time listening to the teacher and then half working on their own. How much time was left?

1 Gemma is having a party. She has £100 to spend. She spends a quarter on drinks and food and half on decorations. How much money does she have left to spend on her birthday cake?

2 On Friday it rained for 60 minutes. The dog was in the garden for two-thirds of the time it rained. How long was he out?

3 Jake is allowed to play on his computer for 80 minutes every day. He spent 20 minutes on it in the morning. What fraction of his time is left for the rest of the day?

Equivalent fraction puzzle

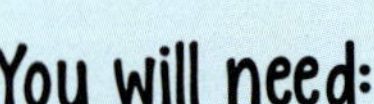

Recognise equivalent fractions

You will need:

- Resource 50: Fraction wall
- scissors

Challenge 1

Use Resource 50: Fraction wall.

1 Cut out the following sections: 1 whole, halves, quarters and eighths.

2 How many different ways can you find to make halves and quarters equal to one whole? Use the fraction wall like a puzzle.

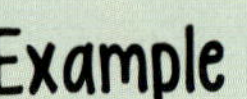

Example

$1 = \frac{1}{2} + \frac{1}{4} + \frac{1}{4}$

Challenge 2

Use Resource 50: Fraction wall.

1 Cut out the following sections: 1 whole, halves, quarters, sixths and eighths.

2 How many equivalent fractions can you find?

Example

$\frac{1}{4} = \frac{1}{8} + \frac{1}{8}$

Challenge 3

Use Resource 50: Fraction wall.

1 Cut out all the sections.

2 How many equivalent fractions can you find?

3 What do you notice about the denominators in the equivalent fractions?

Example

$\frac{1}{3} = \frac{1}{6} + \frac{1}{6}$

Tenths

- Count up and down in tenths
- Find tenths by dividing by 10

This number line is divided into 10 equal parts so they are tenths.

1 Find the missing tenths on the number lines.

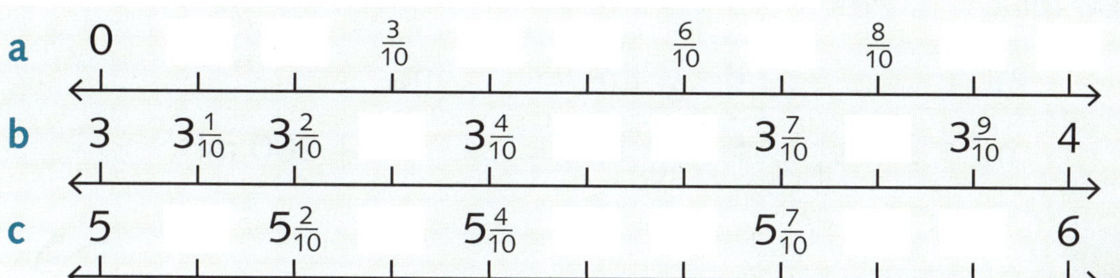

2 10 children want to share these pizzas between them. How many pieces will each of them get?

a

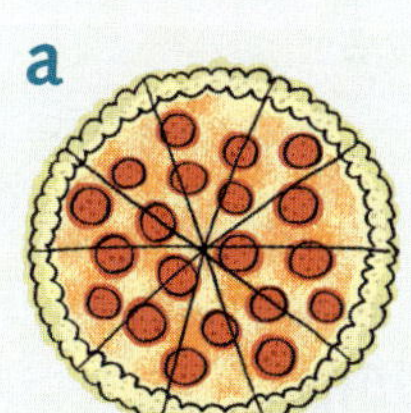

b

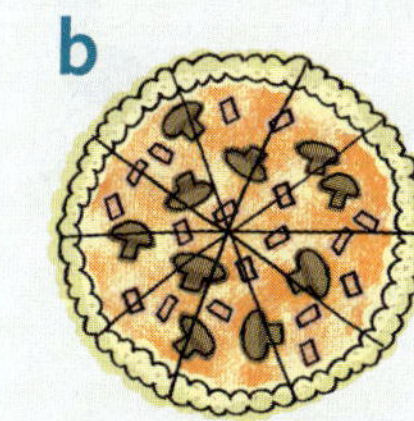

c

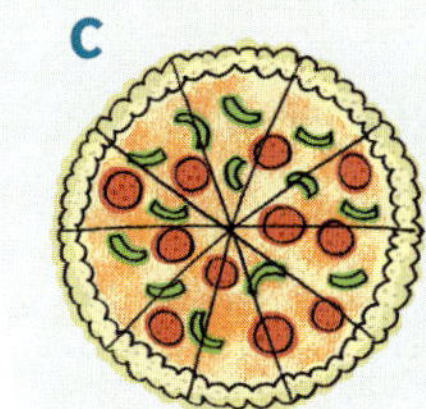

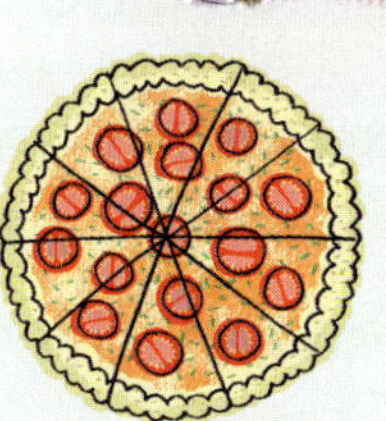

llenge 2

1 Find the missing tenths on the number lines.

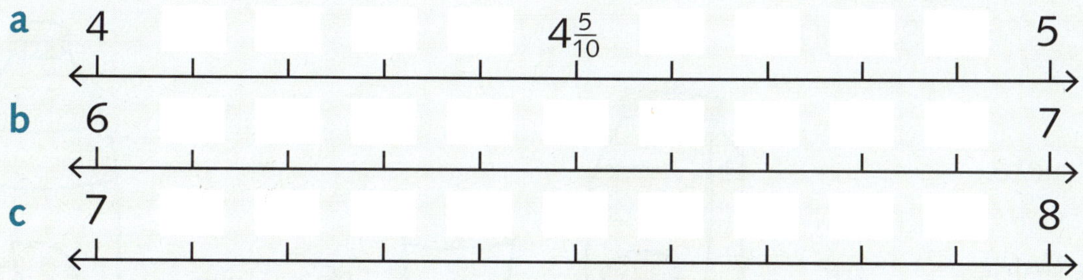

2 Divide these numbers by 10.

a 2 b 5 c 1 d 3 e 4 f 6

nge

Write the tenths that come between these whole numbers.

a 3 and 4 b 14 and 15 c 23 and 24

Fractions of 1 litre

Know how many millilitres are equal to $\frac{1}{2}$, $\frac{1}{4}$, $\frac{3}{4}$ and $\frac{1}{10}$ of 1 litre

Challenge 1

Copy and complete.

a 1 litre = 500 ml + ___ ml

b $\frac{1}{2}$ litre = ___ ml + 250 ml

c $\frac{1}{10}$ litre = ___ ml

d $\frac{1}{4}$ litre = ___ ml

e 500 ml + ___ ml = $\frac{3}{4}$ litre

f $\frac{7}{10}$ litre = ___ ml + 200 ml

Challenge 2

1 Write true or false for each of these statements.

a 500 ml = $\frac{1}{2}$ litre

b $\frac{1}{4}$ litre < 200 ml

c 700 ml < $\frac{3}{4}$ litre

d 100 ml = 1 litre

e $\frac{1}{4}$ litre + $\frac{1}{2}$ litre < 800 ml

f 400 ml > $\frac{1}{2}$ litre

2 Write these capacities in millilitres.

Example

$5l$ 300 ml = 5,000 ml + 300 ml
= 5,300 ml

a $2l$ 500 ml

b $4l$ 250 ml

c $4\frac{1}{4}l$

d $8l$ 600 ml

e $7\frac{1}{2}l$

f $9\frac{3}{4}l$

g $3l$ 900 ml

h $3l$ 400 ml

i $5\frac{3}{4}l$

Challenge 3

1 Copy and complete.

a The carton holds ___ ml of orange juice.

b It will fill ___ glasses.

c It will fill ___ mugs.

1 litre

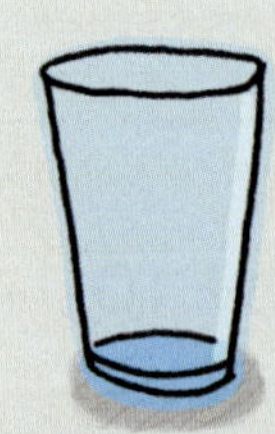

250 ml

200 ml

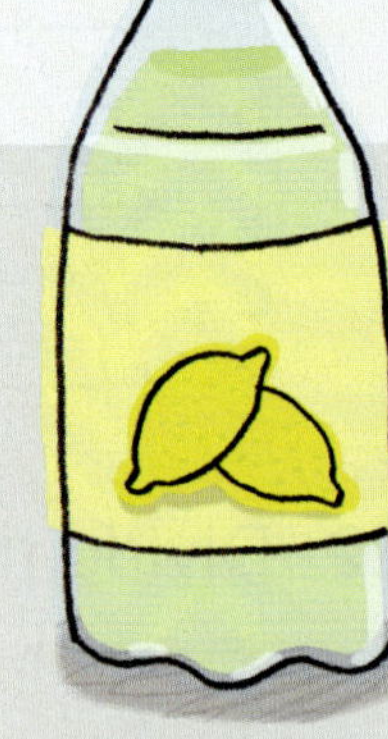

2 litres

2 a The bottle of lemonade holds ___ ml.

b It will fill ___ glasses.

c It will fill ___ mugs.

Millilitres more or less

Read scales to the nearest 100 millilitres

llenges ,2

Write the amount of liquid in each measuring cylinder.

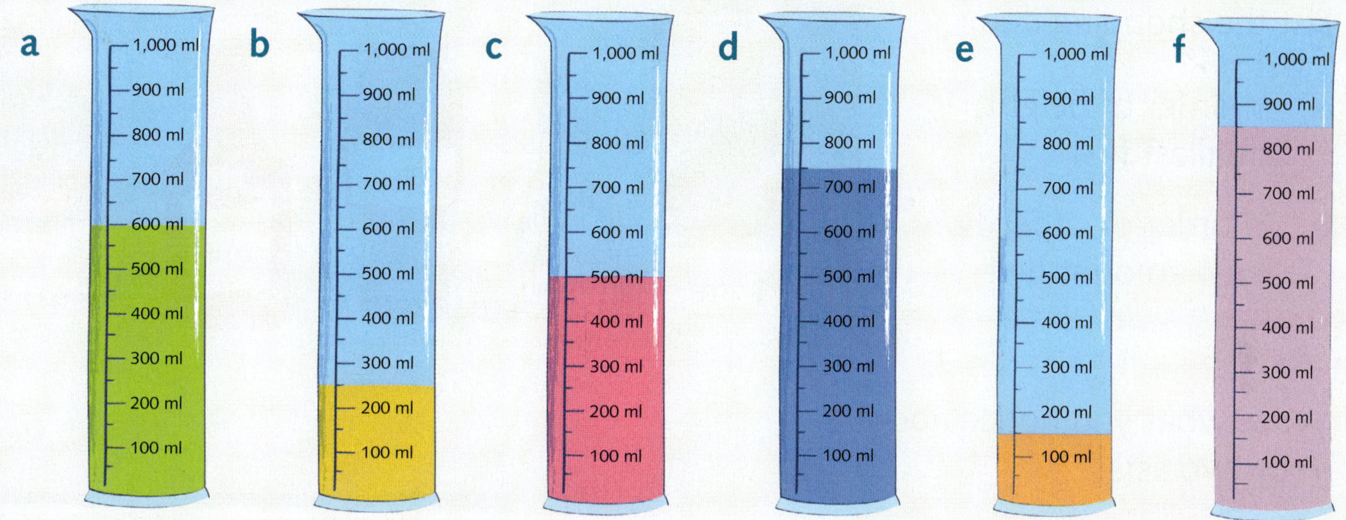

llenge 2

Copy and complete the table for the above cylinders.

	Liquid in cylinder	Amount added	Total amount
a		300 ml	
b	250 ml		700 ml
c		250 ml	
d		150 ml	
e		400 ml	
f		150 ml	

lenge 3

You have three milk jugs. Jug A holds 400 ml, Jug B holds 700 ml and Jug C can hold much more than Jug B. Write how you can use Jugs A and B to measure 1 litre of milk into Jug C.

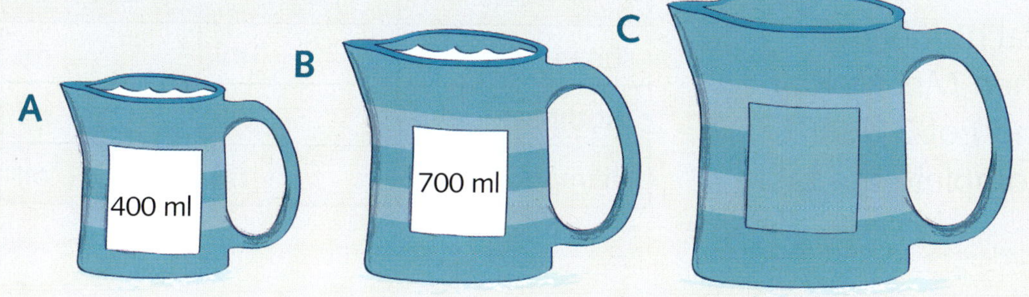

Shopping litres

- Measure and compare capacities
- Use simple scaling of quantities and equivalents of mixed units

You will need:
- ruler

Challenge 1

1 List the shopping items:

a in order of height, smallest first

b in order of capacity, least amount first

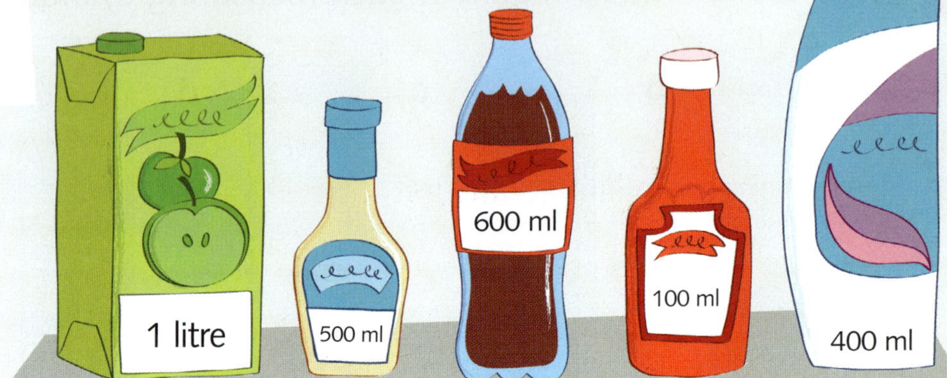

2 Write what you notice about your two lists.

Challenge 2

Look at the poster for Shop 'n' Save. Mrs McKay bought one each of these items and also got one of each item free. How many millilitres of each item did she get altogether?

Shop 'n' Save
Buy 1, get 1 free

tomato sauce	150 ml
olive oil	500 ml
salad dressing	250 ml
orange drink	750 ml
shower gel	300 ml
toothpaste	100 ml
shampoo	400 ml

Challenge 3

Find the total number of millilitres when Mrs McKay bought 2 and got 2 free. Copy and complete the table.

Item	Buy 2	Get 2	Total
shower gel	ml	ml	ml
toothpaste	ml	ml	ml
shampoo	ml	ml	ml

Adding and subtracting capacities

Add and subtract capacities using litres and millilitres

allenge 1

You can pour 5 cups of tea from a 1 litre tea pot. Copy and complete the table.

Number of litres in teapot	1	2	4	5	10
Number of cups	5				

allenge 2

1 How many millilitres altogether in:

a 1 can of lemonade and 1 bottle of orange juice?

b 1 carton of apple juice and 1 can of cola?

2 What is the difference in millilitres between:

a 1 can of lemonade and 1 carton of apple juice?

b 1 bottle of orange juice and 1 can of cola?

150 ml

330 ml

cola

250 ml

270 ml

3 Which drink holds:

a 100 ml more than the carton of apple juice?

b 60 ml less than the can of lemonade?

lenge 3

How much paint is left in each tin when the painter uses:

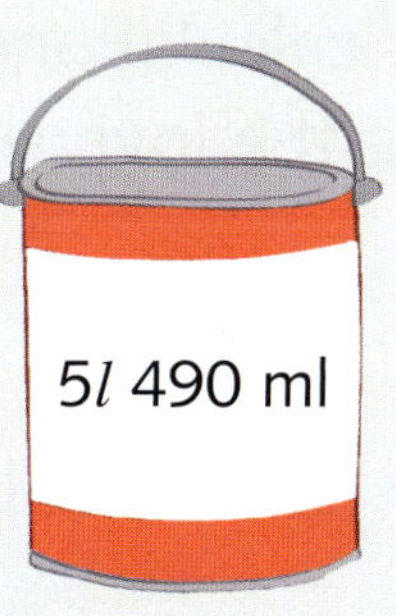

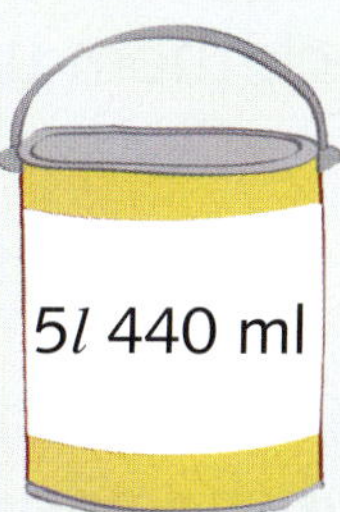

a 4*l* 400 ml of green for the living room ceiling?

b 3*l* 830 ml of yellow for the living room walls?

c 2*l* 750 ml of blue in the kitchen?

d 600 ml of red for the front door?

Estimating and checking column addition

- Add 3-digit numbers using the formal written method of column addition
- Estimate and check the answer to a calculation

Challenge 1

Write an estimate for each calculation and then work out the answer.

a	163 + 234	b	207 + 182	c	364 + 125	d	271 + 218
e	355 + 142	f	257 + 236	g	139 + 246	h	257 + 215

Challenge 2

1 Look at the estimates the children have made for these four calculations.

352 + 241 → Estimate is 600

235 + 202 → Estimate is 300

281 + 395 → Estimate is 500

427 + 241 → Estimate is 650

a Choose one you think is a good estimate and explain why.

b Choose one you think is not a good estimate and explain why.

2 Write an estimate for each calculation and then work out the answer.

a	362 + 219	b	583 + 145	c	457 + 235	d	469 + 228
e	377 + 371	f	408 + 365	g	261 + 573	h	358 + 529

3 Choose three of your calculations in question 2 and check them using the inverse operation.

Challenge 3

1 Do you agree or disagree with Joe? Explain why.

2 Write an estimate for each calculation and then work out the answer.

a	374 + 552	b	461 + 456	c	547 + 417
d	604 + 379	e	763 + 184	f	568 + 218

3 Choose three of your calculations and check them using the inverse operation.

Estimating doesn't help me with my maths.

Addition target answers

- Add 3-digit numbers using the formal written method of column addition
- Estimate and check the answer to a calculation

You will need:
- 1–6 dice

- Make ten 3-digit number add 3-digit number calculations.
- Record your calculations using the formal written method of column addition.

	H	T	O
+			

llenge 1

- For each calculation, write the digit 2 in both the 100s place values.
- Roll the dice four times and decide where to write each digit: either in the 10s or the 1s column.
- Your target is to get an answer as close to **500** as possible.

	H	T	O
	2		
+	2		

llenge 2

- For each calculation, roll the dice six times and decide where to write each digit.
- Your target is to get an answer as close to **500** as possible.

llenge 3

- For each calculation, roll the dice six times and decide where to write each digit.
- Your target is to get an answer as close to **800** as possible.

1 Which calculation has an answer closest to 800?

2 Explain how you decided where to write the digits.

Adding and subtracting money

Add and subtract amounts of money

Challenge 1

Work out the answer to each calculation using your preferred method.

1 a £38 + £45 b £79 + £24 c £58 + £37 d £62 + £51
e £84 + £66 f £135 + £40 g £147 + £50 h £183 + £40

2 a £100 – £57 b £100 – £32 c £100 – £68 d £173 – £40
e £136 – £80 f £200 – £183 g £200 – £124 h £200 – £63

Challenge 2

Work out the answer to each calculation using your preferred method.

1 a £365 + £60 b £382 + £80 c £497 + £90 d £507 + £60
e £553 + £70 f £317 + £242 g £324 + £239 h £472 + £243

2 a £300 – £154 b £400 – £267 c £400 – £96 d £353 – £80
e £457 – £136 f £482 – £135 g £574 – £193 h £673 – £387

Challenge 3

1 Work out the answer to each calculation using your preferred method.

a £473 + £80 b £500 – £271 c £562 – £281 d £473 + £485
e £614 + £90 f £743 – £80 g £500 – £308 h £674 – £158

2 Work out the missing amounts of money.

a £245 + ☐ = £315 b £471 + ☐ = £561 c £326 + ☐ = £726
d ☐ + £50 = £621 e ☐ + £80 = £703 f ☐ + £90 = £754

School shopping

- Add and subtract amounts of money
- Solve problems involving money and reason mathematically

Oscar, Mina and Louis are buying items for their classroom and playground. Work out these money problems. Show your working out.

Oscar has £100.
Mina has £200.
Louis has £500.

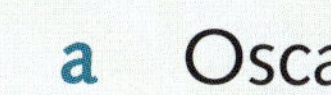

llenge 1

a Oscar buys a bookcase. How much change will he get?

b Mina buys a bookcase and a CD player. How much does she spend?

c Oscar wants to buy a bench. How much more money does he need?

d Mina buys a bench. How much money will she have left?

llenge 2

a Mina wants to buy a bench and a CD player. How much more money does she need?

b Louis buys a tablet. How much change will he get?

c Mina buys the cheapest item in the shop. How much change will she get?

d Mina decides to buy two benches. How much more money will she need?

lenge 3

a Louis buys a tablet and two games. The total cost comes to £479. What was the price of the two games?

b Mina and Louis put their money together and buy a tablet and a laptop. How much change will they get?

c If you had £500 to spend, what items would you buy?

Estimating and checking column subtraction

- Subtract 3-digit numbers using the formal written method of column subtraction
- Estimate and check the answer to a calculation

Write an estimate for each calculation and then work out the answer.

a	274 – 132	**b**	285 – 153	**c**	369 – 127	**d**	356 – 233
e	397 – 242	**f**	373 – 156	**g**	364 – 128	**h**	381 – 215

Challenge 2

1 Look at the estimates the children have made for these four calculations.

a Choose one you think is a good estimate and explain why.

b Choose one you think is not a good estimate and explain why.

391 – 115 → Estimate is 300

432 – 196 → Estimate is 200

285 – 181 → Estimate is 100

466 – 289 → Estimate is 300

2 Write an estimate for each calculation and then work out the answer.

a	374 – 138	**b**	387 – 169	**c**	436 – 282	**d**	453 – 227
e	516 – 362	**f**	584 – 347	**g**	539 – 372	**h**	578 – 269

3 Choose three of your calculations in question 2 and check them using the inverse operation.

Challenge 3

1 Do you agree or disagree with James? Explain why.

Checking my answers is a waste of time.

2 Write an estimate for each calculation and then work out the answer.

a	672 – 317	**b**	648 – 281	**c**	755 – 362
d	784 – 459	**e**	728 – 266	**f**	844 – 137

3 Choose three of your calculations and check them using the inverse operation.

Subtraction target answers

- Subtract 3-digit numbers using the formal written method of column subtraction
- Estimate and check the answer to a calculation

You will need:
- 1–6 dice

- Make ten 3-digit number subtract 3-digit number calculations.
- Record your calculations using the formal written method of column subtraction.
- Make sure that the minuend is larger than the subtrahend.

minuend – subtrahend = difference

- For each calculation, roll the dice six times and decide where to write the digit.
- Your target is to get an answer as close to **100** as possible.

- For each calculation, roll the dice six times and decide where to write the digits.
- Your target is to get an answer as close to **200** as possible.

- For each calculation, roll the dice six times and decide where to write the digits.
- Your target is to get an answer as close to **400** as possible.

1 Which calculation has an answer closest to 400?

2 Explain how you decided where to write the digits.

Jumping forward to the target

Add numbers mentally and use inverse operations to check the answer

addend + addend = sum or total

Draw two empty number lines for each question. Use the number in the blue circle as the start number (an addend) and write it at the beginning. Use the number in the pink circle as the target number (the sum or total) and write it at the end.

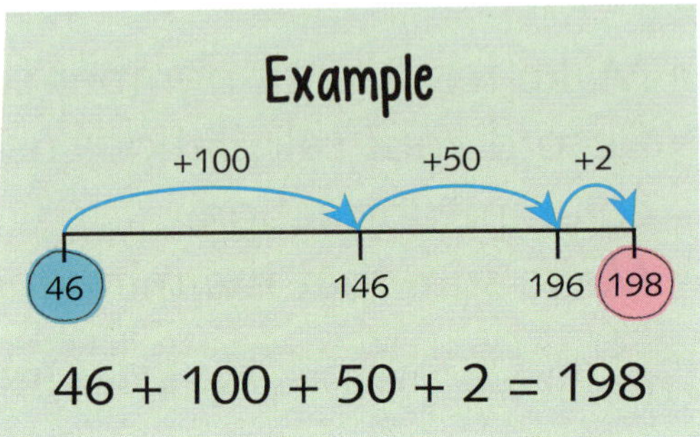

Jump along the number line from the addend to the sum to find the other addend. Your jumps must be in multiples of 100, multiples of 10 or 1s.

Try each one twice doing different jumps. What is the least number of jumps you can do? Write the addition calculation each time.

a 32 89 b 87 142 c 126 187

d 155 243 e 180 265 f 214 296

Challenge 2

1 a 226 298 b 267 352 c 295 423

d 378 499 e 365 421 f 378 494

2 Choose two of your number lines and check your jumps by jumping back.

1 a 357 504 b 381 553 c 405 587

d 437 604 e 516 681 f 525 718

2 Choose two of your number lines and check your answers using subtraction.

Jumping back to the target

Subtract numbers mentally and use inverse operations to check the answer

minuend – subtrahend = difference

Draw two empty number lines for each question. Use the number in the blue circle as the start number (the minuend) and write it at the end. Use the number in the pink circle as the target number (the difference) and write it at the beginning.

Jump back along the number line from the minuend to the difference to find the subtrahend. Your jumps must be in multiples of 100, multiples of 10 or 1s.

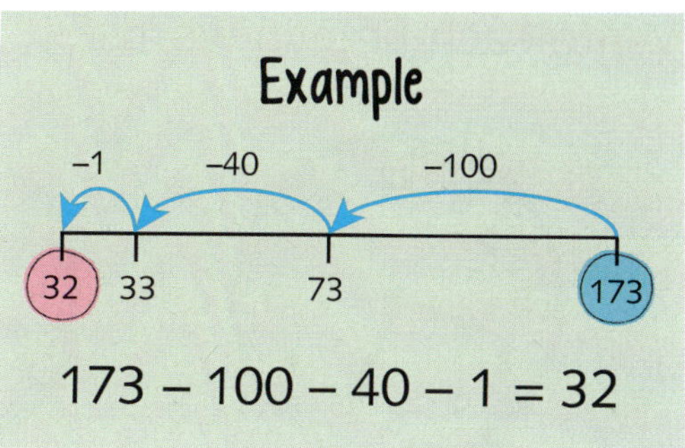

Try each one twice doing different jumps. What is the least number of jumps you can do? Write the subtraction calculation each time.

a 85 41 **b** 136 78 **c** 189 147

d 241 162 **e** 266 174 **f** 324 251

lenge 2

1 **a** 286 203 **b** 336 257 **c** 374 281

d 497 368 **e** 451 332 **f** 522 354

2 Choose two of your number lines and check your jumps by jumping forwards between the numbers.

1 **a** 487 374 **b** 507 352 **c** 568 433

d 612 449 **e** 680 526 **f** 723 555

2 Choose two of your number lines and check your answers using addition.

Just a minute

Read and write the time to the minute on 12-hour analogue and digital clocks

Challenge 1

Write each time in words.

a

b

c

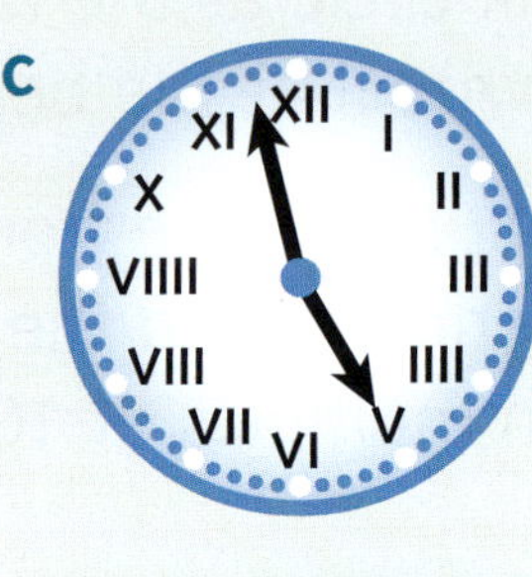

Example

16 minutes past 12

d 3:34

e 5:17

f 7:03

Challenge 2

1 Write the digital time to match each time below.

a	13 minutes past 6	**b**	5 past 8	**c**	22 minutes to 2
d	six forty-six	**e**	10 to 10	**f**	18 minutes to 1

Example

12 minutes to 4
3:48

2 Write these digital times 20 minutes later.

a	3:16	**b**	8:08	**c**	9:36
d	1:12	**e**	11:24	**f**	10:42

Challenge 3

The time this clock shows is 11:37.
Write in digital form the time it will show:

a	in 2 hours' time	**b**	in half an hour's time
c	18 minutes later	**d**	48 minutes later

Race times

Use seconds, minutes and hours to estimate, compare and measure time

allenge 1

Choose the most likely time estimate for each of these activities.

a	boiling an egg	2 minutes	5 minutes	30 minutes
b	opening a birthday present	15 minutes	1 minute	15 seconds
c	getting to school in the morning	3 minutes	30 minutes	3 hours
d	flying from London to Florida	1 hour	20 hours	9 hours

allenge 2

Each sheep dog must finish in less than 1 minute to qualify for the finals.

1 Write the names and the times, in minutes and seconds, of the non-qualifiers.

2 What is the difference in seconds between the fastest and the slowest sheep dog?

Sheep dog results	
Name	**Time in seconds**
Fly	71
Scot	48
Rex	62
Jenny	66
Bruce	53
Meg	57

llenge 3

The 10 km run started at 2:30 p.m.

1 Write the time the digital finishing clock showed for each runner.

2 Who won the race?

3 Who was last?

4 How much faster was Alan than Jan?

5 How many minutes slower than the winner was Flo?

10 km results	
Name	**Minutes**
Alan	50
Flo	62
Pat	47
Jan	64
Kit	58

Using a calendar

Know the number of days in each month and year

Challenge 1

1 Copy and complete.

a ☐ days in 1 week   b ☐ months in 1 year   c ☐ days in 1 year

2 Write which months have:

a 30 days   b 31 days   c less than 30 days

Challenge 2

1 Look at the calendar page for May 2024.
Write the day of the week for:

a 14th May   b 23rd May
c 27th May   d 5th May
e the first day in May   f the first day in June
g 30th April

MAY 2024						
S	M	T	W	Th	F	S
			1	2	3	4
5	6	7	8	9	10	11
12	13	14	15	16	17	18
19	20	21	22	23	24	25
26	27	28	29	30	31	

2 a The year 2020 was a leap year. Draw a time line to show the leap years from 2020 to 2040.

b 2024 is a leap year. Write the date for the 60th day of 2024.

Challenge 3

1 Four friends will be 8 years old in May 2024.
Write the date of each friend's birthday.

Brian: first Monday   **Clare**: second Friday
Darren: third Saturday   **Emma**: last Wednesday

2 How many days older is:

a Brian than Clare?   b Clare than Darren?   c Darren than Emma?

Cycle race times

Find the time taken to complete a task or event

llenge 1

Scottish shortbread takes 25 minutes to bake.
Mr Fraser the baker puts trays of shortbread into his oven at these times.

a 7:20 a.m. **b** 7:55 a.m. **c** 8:13 a.m. **d** 8:48 a.m.

Work out the finish time for each tray of shortbread.

llenge 2

Using the table, work out the finish time for each cyclist in Stage 2 of the Tour of Scotland Cycle Race.

Cyclist	Start time	Time for Stage 2: hours	Time for Stage 2: minutes	Finish time
1	2:45	2	14	
2	2:45	1	55	
3	2:45	2	19	
4	2:50	1	59	
5	2:50	1	52	
6	2:50	2	13	

enge 3

1 Using the table, work out how long each cyclist took to complete the time trial part of the race.

2 Write the cyclists in order of finishing the time trial, winner first.

Cyclist	Start time	Finish time
1	10.30	12:40
2	10:33	12:28
3	10:36	12:35
4	10:39	12:45
5	10:42	12:32
6	10:45	12:38

Multiplication using the expanded written method

Use the expanded written method to calculate TO × O

Challenge 1

Choose ten numbers from the circles above. Write the multiples of 10 that each number comes between.

Example

70 ← 74 → 80

Challenge 2

Choose six numbers from the circles above. Multiply two numbers by 3, two numbers by 4 and two numbers by 8. Estimate the answer first, then use the expanded written method to work out the answer.

Example

86 × 4 → 90 × 4 = 360

	8	6	
×		4	
	2	4	(6 × 4)
3	2	0	(80 × 4)
3	4	4	

Challenge 3

Multiply the two numbers alongside each other in the bottom row together to find the number above in the second row. Multiply the two numbers in the second row together to find the number at the top. Calculate the answers mentally for as long as you are able, then use the expanded written method.

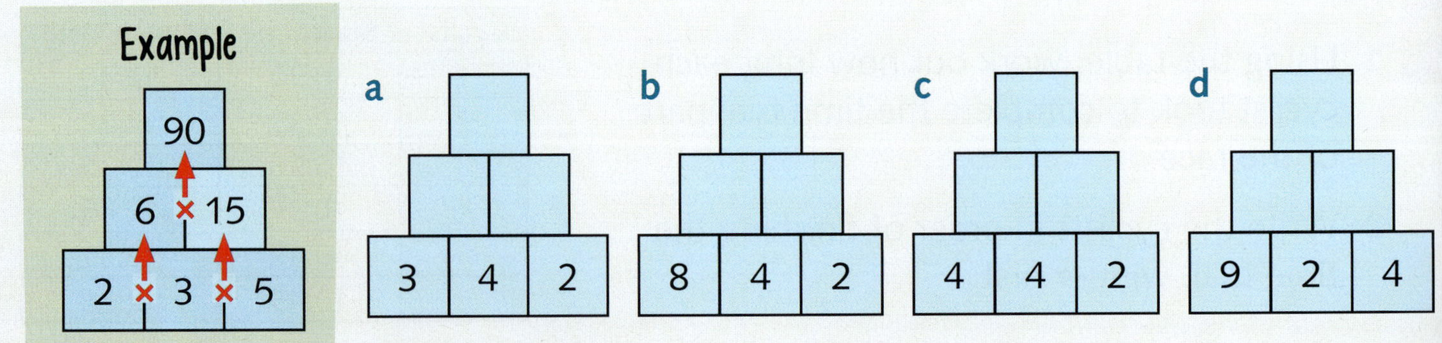

Multiplication: Introducing the formal written method (1)

Use the formal written method to calculate TO × O

Challenges 1,2

Estimate the answer to each calculation.

a 37 × 4	b 54 × 4	c 69 × 3	d 34 × 8	e 76 × 3
f 48 × 4	g 55 × 5	h 88 × 8	i 76 × 3	j 87 × 5

Challenge 2

Find the answer to each of the calculations in Challenges 1,2 using the formal written method of multiplication. Check your answer is close to your estimated answer.

Example

86 × 4 ⟶ 90 × 4 = 360

$$\begin{array}{r} 86 \\ \times \quad {}_{2}4 \\ \hline 344 \\ \hline \end{array}$$

Challenge 3

The children used number cards and a spinner with the numbers 2, 3, 4, 5, 8 and 10 to make some calculations. They worked out the answers. Sam forgot to write the number from the spinner in each of his calculations. Can you work out which number he spun each time?

a 63 × ☐ = 252

b 57 × ☐ = 228

c 37 × ☐ = 296

d 83 × ☐ = 664

e 76 × ☐ = 304

f 76 × ☐ = 380

Multiplication: Introducing the formal written method (2)

Use the formal written method to calculate TO × O

Challenge 1

Write how much it would cost to buy:

40p each	50p each	20p each	80p/bunch	£1/slice	30p each

a 6 **b** 5 **c** 3 **d** 4

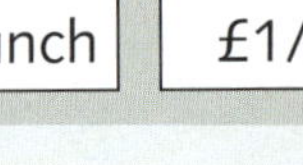

e 7 **f** 6 **g** 8 **h** 5

Challenge 2

For each box of fruit, spin the spinner and write a multiplication calculation. Estimate the answer first. Then use the formal written method to calculate the answer.

You will need:

- Resource 36: 2, 3, 4, 5, 8 and 10 spinner

Example

$58 \times 8 \rightarrow 60 \times 8 = 480$

$$\begin{array}{r} 5\ 8 \\ \times\ \ _{6}8 \\ \hline 4\ 6\ 4 \\ \hline \end{array}$$

Challenge 3

Solve these word problems using the pictures in Challenge 2.

1. The green grocer sells 8 boxes of apples and 5 boxes of oranges in a week. Which fruit does he sell more of? How many more?
2. There are 24 watermelon quarters. How many full watermelons would this be?
3. 8 boxes of lemons and 4 boxes of grapes are sold in a week. How many lemons and bunches of grapes is this altogether?
4. There are 4 boxes of bananas to sell. Each box has 5 rotten bananas which are thrown out. What is the total number of bananas that can be sold?

Solving word problems (8)

Solve word problems and reason mathematically

llenge 1 Write in the missing sign.

a $4 ★ 6 = 24$ b $32 ★ 8 = 4$ c $30 = 6 ★ 5$ d $6 ★ 8 = 14$

e $72 = 9 ★ 8$ f $29 ★ 8 = 21$ g $15 ★ 3 = 12$ h $88 ★ 11 = 8$

llenge 2 Write how much it would cost to buy:

a 2

b 3 sets of 

c 2 sets of

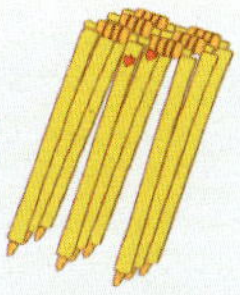

d 2  and 1

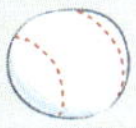

e 3

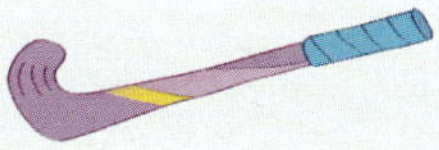

f 4 

lenge 3 Answer these questions about the sports equipment in Challenge 2.

1 The school buys 30 hockey sticks. How much do they spend?

2 What is the difference in cost between a football and a basketball?

3 What is the cost of 5 sets of tennis balls?

4 Tennis balls are sold in packs of 3. How much would 1 tennis ball cost?

5 The sports shop has sold out of tennis racquets. Tennis racquets cost 4 times more than a set of tennis balls. What is the cost of a tennis racquet?

6 How much do 8 basketballs cost?

7 Jay has £100 to spend. Can he buy 3 basketballs? Explain why or why not.

Division using partitioning

Use partitioning to calculate TO ÷ O

Find the multiples of 30, 40, 50 and 80.

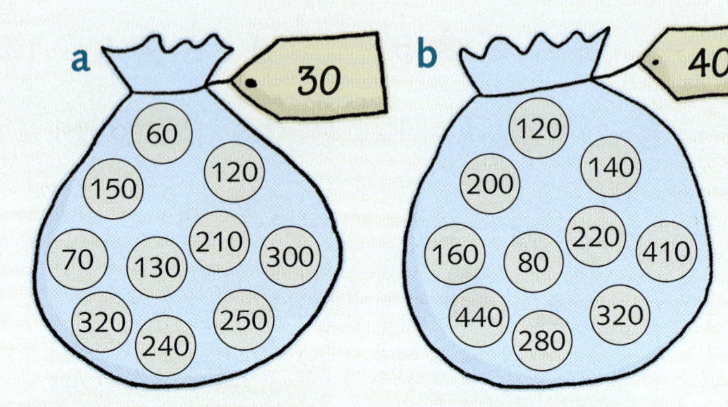

c 50

130, 150, 50, 200, 220, 100, 180, 350, 400, 420

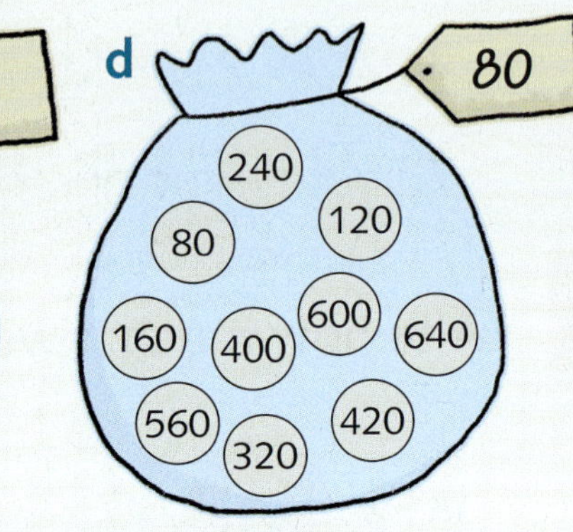

Challenge 2

1	a	9 ÷ 3 =
	b	90 ÷ 3 =
2	a	8 ÷ 4 =
	b	80 ÷ 4 =
3	a	16 ÷ 4 =
	b	160 ÷ 4 =
4	a	15 ÷ 3 =
	b	150 ÷ 3 =
5	a	10 ÷ 5 =
	b	100 ÷ 5 =
6	a	6 ÷ 2 =
	b	60 ÷ 2 =
7	a	4 ÷ 4 =
	b	40 ÷ 4 =
8	a	8 ÷ 2 =
	b	80 ÷ 2 =
9	a	12 ÷ 4 =
	b	120 ÷ 4 =
10	a	32 ÷ 8 =
	b	320 ÷ 8 =
11	a	24 ÷ 4 =
	b	240 ÷ 4 =
12	a	18 ÷ 3 =
	b	180 ÷ 3 =

Challenge 3

Partition each of these numbers to help you find the answer to the division calculation.

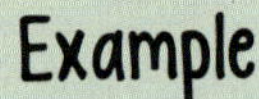

Example

69 → 60, 9

60 ÷ 3 → 20; 9 ÷ 3 → 3

20 + 3 = 23

69 ÷ 3 = (60 ÷ 3) + (9 ÷ 3)
= 20 + 3
= 23

a 88 ÷ 2 b 84 ÷ 4

c 63 ÷ 3 d 48 ÷ 2

e 66 ÷ 3 f 86 ÷ 2 g 88 ÷ 4 h 96 ÷ 3 i 68 ÷ 2 j 76 ÷ 4

Division using the expanded written method

Use the expanded written method to calculate TO ÷ O

Challenge 1

Write five multiples of each of these numbers.

20

Example

30 → 90, 120, 270...

Challenge 2

1 Choose three numbers. Divide each number by 3 using the expanded written method of division. Estimate the answer first.

75 54 81

Example

72 ÷ 3 → 60 ÷ 3 = 20

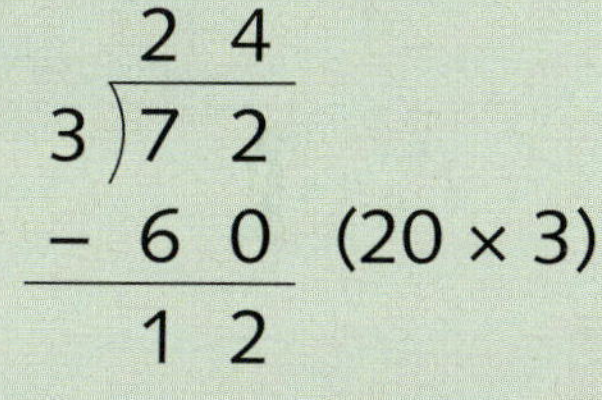

```
    2 4
 3 )7 2
  - 6 0  (20 × 3)
    1 2
  - 1 2  (4 × 3)
      0
```

2 Choose three numbers. Divide each number by 5 using the expanded written method of division. Estimate the answer first.

65 80 60 75 90 85

3 Choose three numbers. Divide each number by 2 using the expanded written method of division. Estimate the answer first.

34

56 38 50 92

4 Check one of your answers from each set using the inverse operation. Choose the method of multiplication you find the easiest.

Challenge 3

One of the calculations in each set is the odd one out. Can you find it? Explain why it is the odd one.

a 96 ÷ 4
72 ÷ 3
85 ÷ 5
48 ÷ 2

b 68 ÷ 4
81 ÷ 3
74 ÷ 2
95 ÷ 5

Division using the formal written method

Use the formal written method to calculate TO ÷ O

Challenge 1

Write the division fact for each number coming out of the machine.

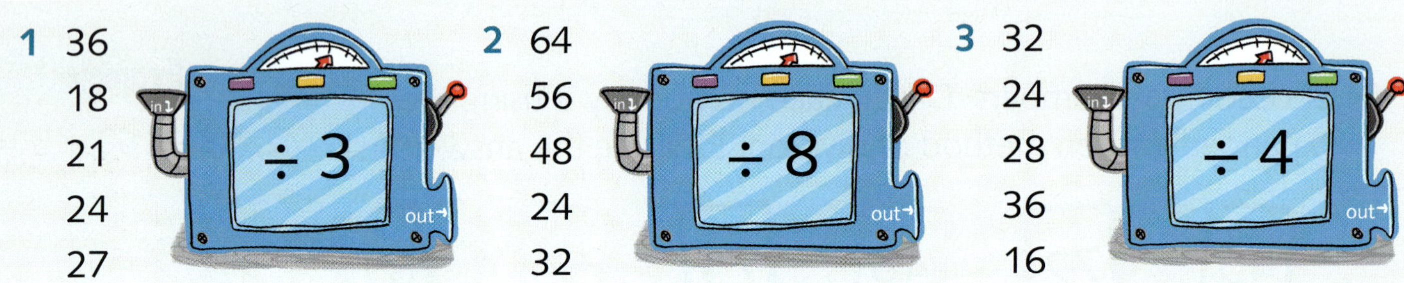

Challenges 2, 3

Estimate the answer to each calculation.

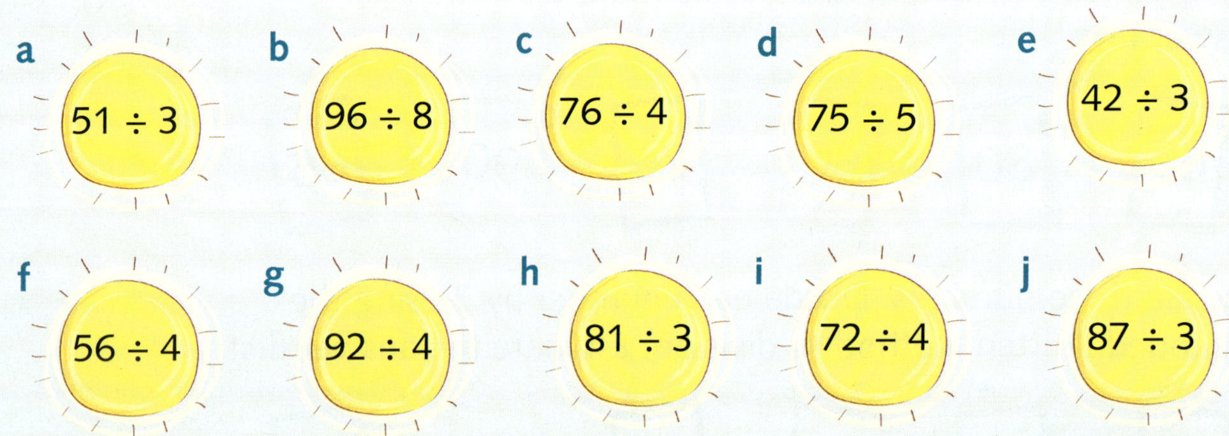

Challenge 3

1 Find the answer to each of the calculations in Challenge 2 using the formal written method of division.

2 Check three of your answers using the inverse operation. Choose the method of multiplication you find the easiest.

Example

  2 4
3)7 ¹2

Example

$24 \times 3 = (20 \times 3) + (4 \times 3)$
$= 60 + 12$
$= 72$

Solving word problems (9)

Solve word problems and reason mathematically

Match the division fact with its answer.

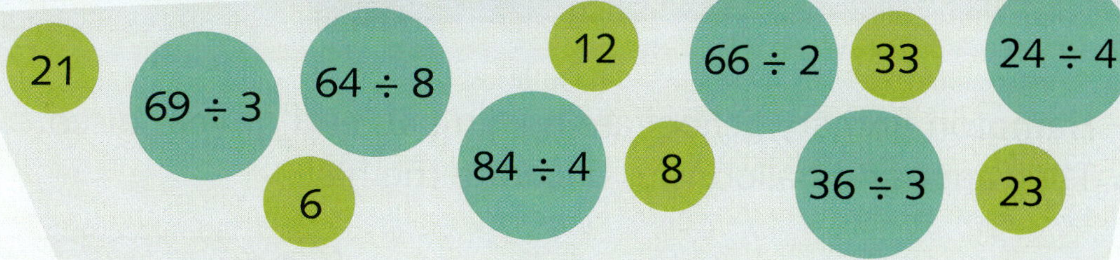

1 The Year 3 children had a summer picnic. Use the pictures to solve the problems.

a The sandwiches were shared equally between 3 groups. How many sandwiches per group?

b The samosas were shared equally between 5 groups. How many samosas per group?

c The cartons of fruit juice were divided equally amongst 2 classes. How many per class?

d 3 boxes of watermelon slices were eaten. How many slices altogether?

e The cook made another 4 boxes of sandwiches. How many more sandwiches did she make?

f The ice creams were divided between 4 classes. How many children in each class received an ice cream?

g There were 96 children at the picnic. How many children did not receive a carton of fruit juice?

2 Choose three of your calculations and check your answer using the inverse operation.

Use the pictures above to make up your own word problems using these calculations.

a $72 \times 3 =$

b $96 \div 8 =$

c $85 + 72 =$

d $96 - 48 =$

School disco pictograms

Show data in a pictogram where a picture represents 2 or 5 units

You will need:
- squared paper
- ruler

Hampton Primary School are holding an end of year disco. They are using balloons to decorate the hall.

1 Copy the Colour and Frequency columns.

Then count the tally marks and complete the Frequency column.

Colour	Tally	Frequency
red	𝍸 𝍸 𝍸 |	
orange	𝍸 𝍸	
green	𝍸	
yellow	𝍸 𝍸 ||	
blue	𝍸 ||	

2 Using the table, copy and complete the pictogram. Use a circle ○ to represent 2 balloons.

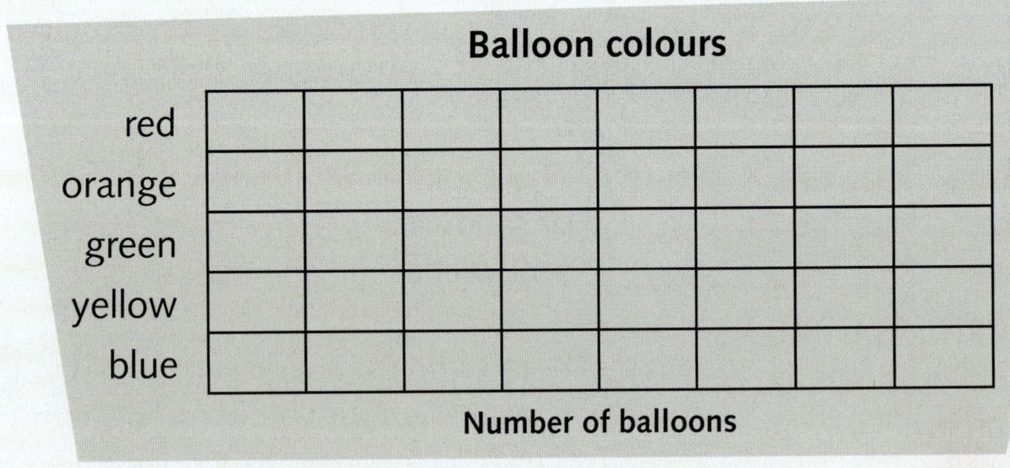

Key

○ = 2 balloons

3 How many balloons are:

a orange? **b** yellow? **c** blue?

4 Which colour of balloon is:

a most common? **b** least common?

5 How many balloons are there altogether?

llenges 2,3

Year 4 have collected money to pay for the disco.

1 Count the coins and notes.

Copy and complete the frequency table below.

Note/Coin	Frequency
£10	
£5	
£2	
£1	
50p	

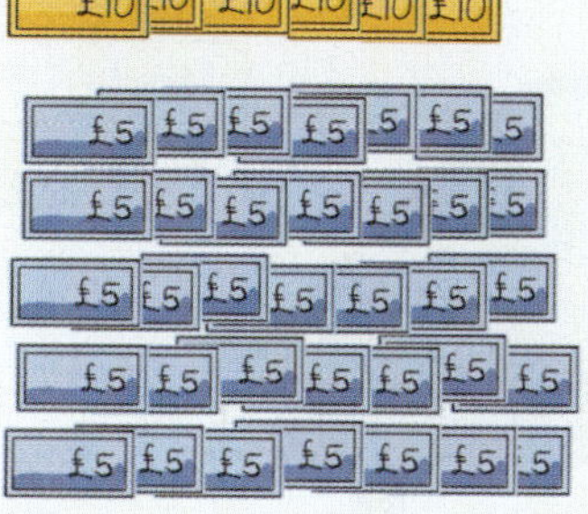

You will need:
- squared paper
- ruler

2 Copy and complete the pictogram.

Coins and notes

£10								
£5								
£2								
£1								
50p								

Number of notes or coins

Key

○ = 5 notes or coins

a How many notes are there?

b How many coins are there?

c How many fewer £10 notes are there than £5 notes?

d How many fewer £2 coins are there than £1 coins?

lenge 3

How much money was collected altogether at the school disco? Show all your working out.

Activities bar charts

Show data in a bar chart with intervals labelled in 5s or 10s

Peter potted these balls on a pool table.

Colour	Number
Black	2
Blue	11
Green	9
Red	8
Yellow	4

You will need:

- squared paper
- ruler

1 Copy and complete the bar chart using the data in the table.

2 Which colour of ball was potted:

a the most?

b the least?

3 How many more blue balls did Peter pot than:

a black? b green?

c red? d yellow?

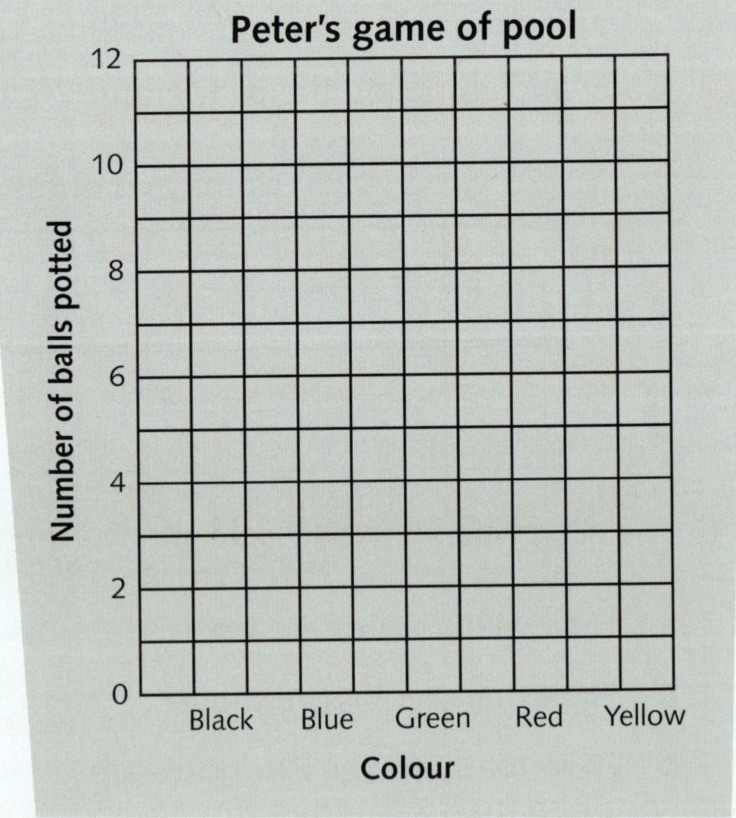

4 How many balls did he pot altogether?

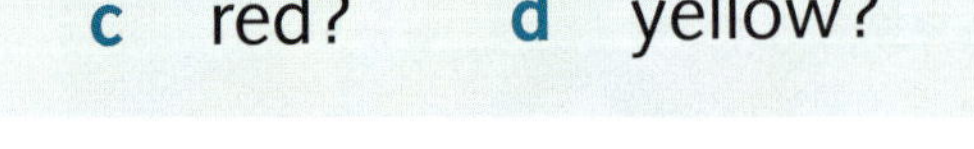

allenge 2

This table shows the number of children who go to after school activities.

Activity	Number
Computers	25
Football skills	30
Games	20
Gymnastics	15
Painting	10

1 Copy and complete the bar chart using the data in the table.

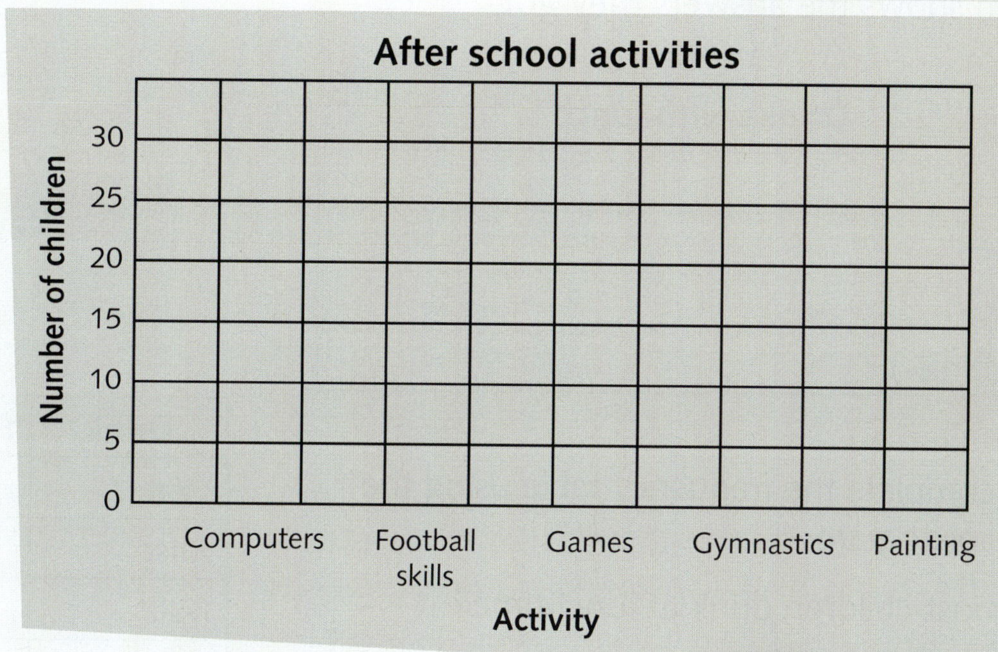

2 What does the tallest bar show?

3 Which activity is twice as popular as:

a Gymnastics? b Painting?

4 How many more children choose Computers than:

a Gymnastics? b Games?

5 How many children go to after school activities?

lenge 3

Using each word or phrase only once, write five statements about the data in Challenges 1 and 2.

most	difference	fewer
least popular	less	

On the menu pictograms

Answer questions about data in scaled pictograms and tables

Class 3A asked those children that have school lunches, "What do you drink with your lunch?"
The pictogram shows the answers they got.

You will need:
- ruler

Key
[glass] = 5 children

Drink	Frequency
Water	
Juice	
Milk	
Nothing	

1 Copy and complete the frequency table using the data in the pictogram.

2 What do most children drink at lunchtime?

3 How many children have:

a juice? b milk? c nothing to drink with their meal?

4 How many more children drink water than:

a juice? b milk?

5 How many children took part in the survey?

Class 3A asked, "Which do you prefer to eat with your main course?" The pictogram shows their results.

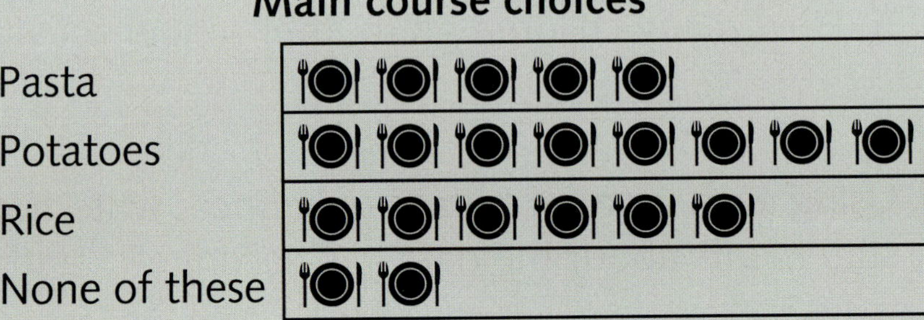

Key [plate] = 5 children

1 How many children prefer:

a pasta? b potatoes? c rice? d none of these?

2 How many more children prefer potatoes to:

a pasta? b rice?

3 How many fewer children prefer pasta to rice?

4 How many children altogether took part in Class 3A's survey?

allenge 3

Class 3A asked, "What is your favourite pudding?"
The pictogram shows their results.

You will need:
- squared paper
- ruler

1 Draw a pictogram for the favourite puddings using the key: = 4 children.

2 Imagine that you are the school cook.

a Which pudding would you remove from the menu? Give a reason for your answer.

b What pudding might you put in its place?

3 Work with a partner. Choose three or four puddings from the pictogram. Ask the children in your class to say which of them is their favourite pudding. Record your results in a pictogram.

Off to Italy bar charts

This bar chart shows the number of holiday flights to Italy from a UK airport.

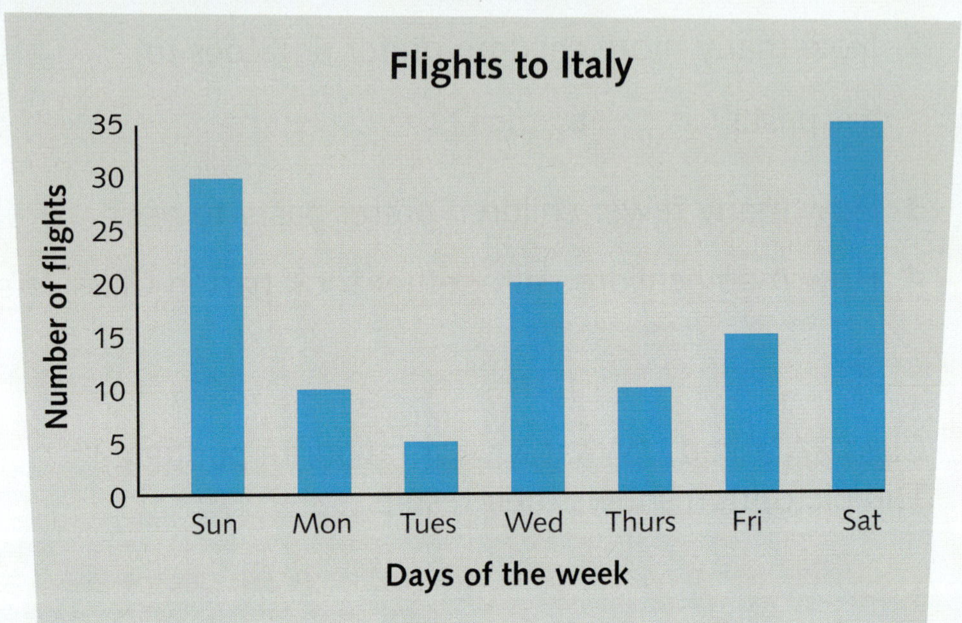

1 How many flights to Italy were:

- a on Sunday?
- b on Tuesday?
- c on Friday?
- d on Saturday?

2 Which two days had the same number of flights?

3 Which day had:

- a five more flights than Sunday?
- b ten fewer flights than Sunday?

4 Why do you think that Saturday was the busiest day?

5 How many holiday flights were there altogether?

allenge 2

The bar chart shows the colours of the cars for hire at the airport in Italy.

Colour of hire cars

Number of cars: 0, 10, 20, 30, 40, 50, 60, 70, 80

Colour: Black, Blue, Red, Silver, White

1 Which colour of car is:

a the most common?

b the least common?

c twice as common as blue?

d half as common as silver?

2 How many more cars are white than:

a black? b silver?

3 How many cars are there altogether?

4 The table shows how many tourists each gondolier carried in one week.

Write three questions about the table for your partner to answer.

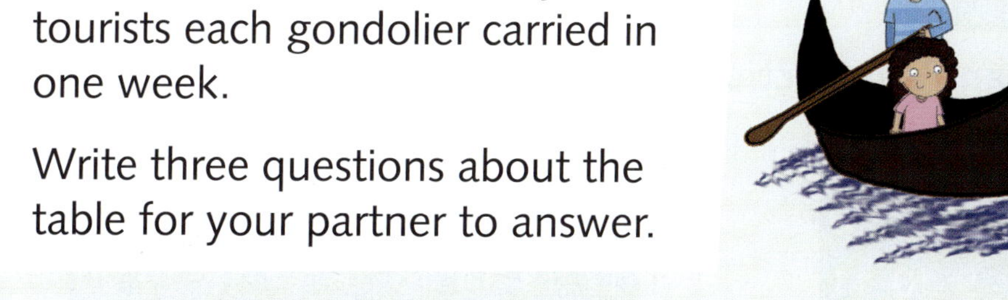

Gondolier	Number
Alberto	25
Enzo	45
Luigi	30
Marco	55
Nico	40

llenge 3

Work with a partner. Make a survey by asking at least 20 children, "Which of these is your favourite Italian food?"

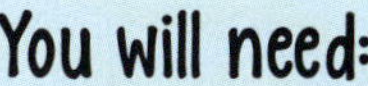

You will need:

- squared paper
- ruler

a Draw a tally chart and list the foods:

spaghetti, lasagne, pizza, macaroni and ice cream.

b Draw a bar chart of your results.

Maths facts

Problem solving

The seven steps to solving word problems

1 Read the problem carefully. 2 What do you have to find?
3 What facts are given? 4 Which of the facts do you need? 5 Make a plan.
6 Carry out your plan to obtain your answer. 7 Check your answer.

Number and place value

100	200	300	400	500	600	700	800	900
10	20	30	40	50	60	70	80	90
1	2	3	4	5	6	7	8	9

Addition and subtraction

Addition and subtraction facts to 10 and 20

+	0	1	2	3	4	5	6	7	8	9	10
0	0	1	2	3	4	5	6	7	8	9	10
1	1	2	3	4	5	6	7	8	9	10	11
2	2	3	4	5	6	7	8	9	10	11	12
3	3	4	5	6	7	8	9	10	11	12	13
4	4	5	6	7	8	9	10	11	12	13	14
5	5	6	7	8	9	10	11	12	13	14	15
6	6	7	8	9	10	11	12	13	14	15	16
7	7	8	9	10	11	12	13	14	15	16	17
8	8	9	10	11	12	13	14	15	16	17	18
9	9	10	11	12	13	14	15	16	17	18	19
10	10	11	12	13	14	15	16	17	18	19	20

+	11	12	13	14	15	16	17	18	19	20
0	11	12	13	14	15	16	17	18	19	20
1	12	13	14	15	16	17	18	19	20	
2	13	14	15	16	17	18	19	20		
3	14	15	16	17	18	19	20			
4	15	16	17	18	19	20				
5	16	17	18	19	20					
6	17	18	19	20						
7	18	19	20							
8	19	20								
9	20									

Multiples of 10 addition and subtraction facts

+	0	10	20	30	40	50	60	70	80	90	100
0	0	10	20	30	40	50	60	70	80	90	100
10	10	20	30	40	50	60	70	80	90	100	110
20	20	30	40	50	60	70	80	90	100	110	120
30	30	40	50	60	70	80	90	100	110	120	130
40	40	50	60	70	80	90	100	110	120	130	140
50	50	60	70	80	90	100	110	120	130	140	150
60	60	70	80	90	100	110	120	130	140	150	160
70	70	80	90	100	110	120	130	140	150	160	170
80	80	90	100	110	120	130	140	150	160	170	180
90	90	100	110	120	130	140	150	160	170	180	190
100	100	110	120	130	140	150	160	170	180	190	200

Written methods – addition

Example: 548 + 387

Expanded written method

```
  5 4 8
+ 3 8 7
-------
    1 5
  1 2 0
  8 0 0
-------
  9 3 5
```

Formal written method

```
  5 4 8
+ 3 8 7
-------
  9 3 5
-------
  1 1
```

Written methods – subtraction

Example: 582 – 237

Expanded written method

```
          70     12
     500  8̸0     2̸
  –  200  30     7
  -----------------
     300  40     5
```

300 + 40 + 5 = 345

Formal written method

```
      7   1
    5 8̸  2
  – 2 3  7
  --------
    3 4  5
```

You can also write the exchanged values like this.

```
      7 12
    5 8̸ 2
  – 2 3 7
  -------
    3 4 5
```

Multiplication and division

Multiplication and division facts

×	2	3	4	5	8	10
1	2	3	4	5	8	10
2	4	6	8	10	16	20
3	6	9	12	15	24	30
4	8	12	16	20	32	40
5	10	15	20	25	40	50
6	12	18	24	30	48	60
7	14	21	28	35	56	70
8	16	24	32	40	64	80
9	18	27	36	45	72	90
10	20	30	40	50	80	100
11	22	33	44	55	88	110
12	24	36	48	60	96	120

Multiples of 10 multiplication and division facts

×	1	2	3	4	5	6	7	8	9	10	11	12
20	20	40	60	80	100	120	140	160	180	200	220	240
30	30	60	90	120	150	180	210	240	270	300	330	360
40	40	80	120	160	200	240	280	320	360	400	440	480
50	50	100	150	200	250	300	350	400	450	500	550	600
80	80	160	240	320	400	480	560	640	720	800	880	960
100	100	200	300	400	500	600	700	800	900	1,000	1,100	1,200

Written methods – division

Example: 92 ÷ 4

Partitioning

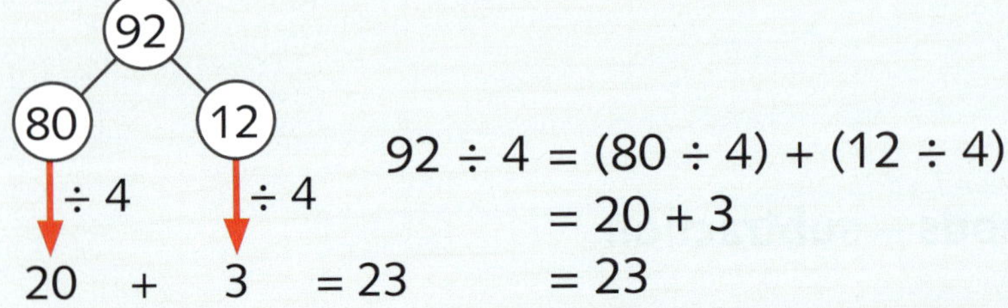

Expanded written method

```
    2 3
 4 )9 2
  - 8 0   (20 × 4)
    1 2
  - 1 2   (3 × 4)
      0
```

You can also include the related multiplication facts.

Formal written method

```
     2  3
 4 ) 9 ¹2
```

Written methods – multiplication

Example: 63 × 8

Partitioning

$63 \times 8 = (60 \times 8) + (3 \times 8)$
$= 480 + 24$
$= 504$

Grid method

×	60	3	
8	480	24	= 504

Expanded written method

```
    6 3
 ×    8
    2 4   (3 × 8)
  4 8 0   (60 × 8)
  5 0 4
  1
```

Formal written method

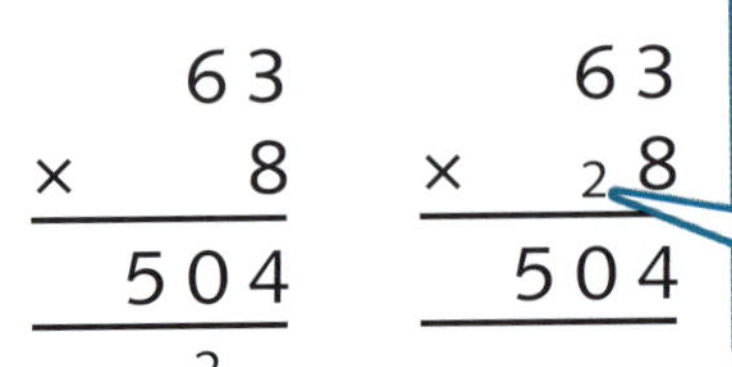

```
    6 3          6 3
 ×    8      ×  ₂8
  5 0 4        5 0 4
    2
```

You can also write the regrouped value like this.

Fractions

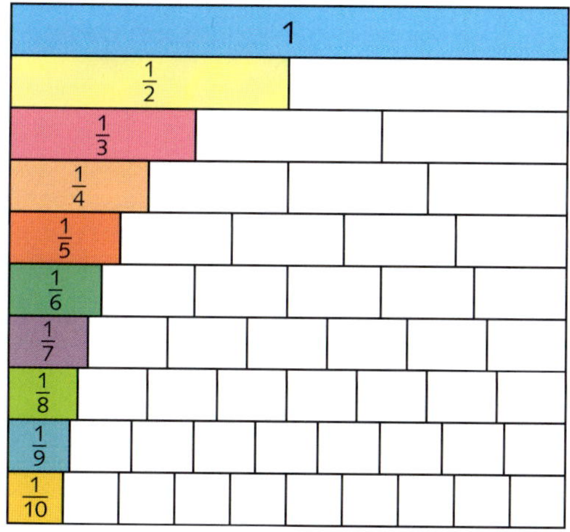

Measurement

Length

1 metre (m) = 100 centimetres (cm) = 1,000 millimetres (mm)

Mass

1 kilogram (kg) = 1,000 grams (g)

Capacity

1 litre (*l*) = 1,000 millilitres (ml)

Time

1 year	=	12 months
	=	365 days
	=	366 days (leap year)
1 week	=	7 days
1 day	=	24 hours
1 hour	=	60 minutes
1 minute	=	60 seconds

12-hour clock

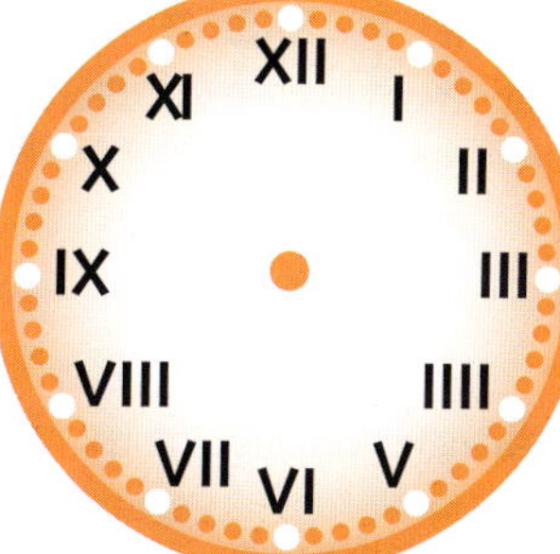

24-hour clock

Properties of shape

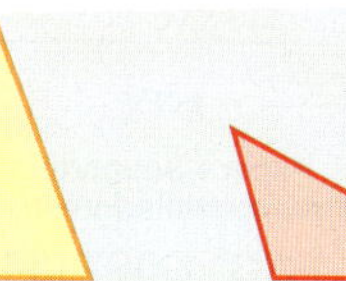

right-angled triangle

equilateral triangle

isosceles triangle

scalene triangle

circle

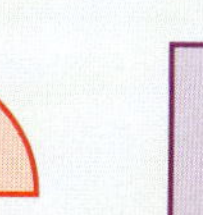

semi-circle

square

rectangle

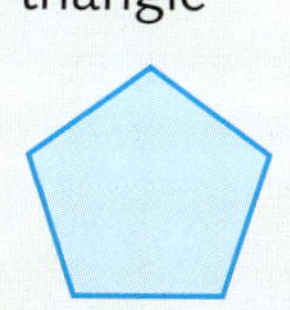

pentagon

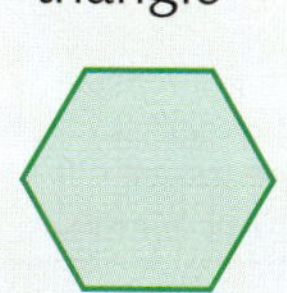

hexagon

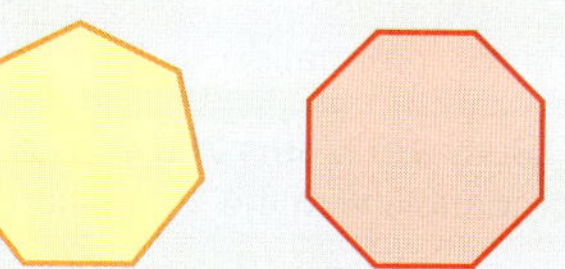

heptagon

octagon

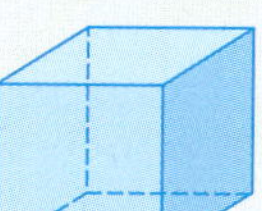

cube

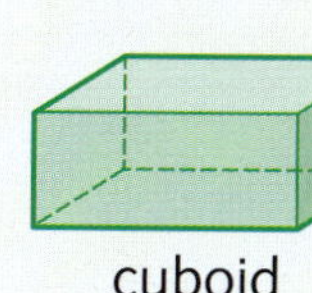

cuboid

cone

cylinder

sphere

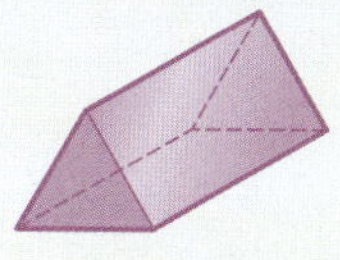
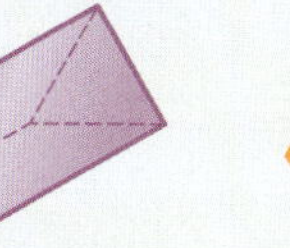

triangular prism

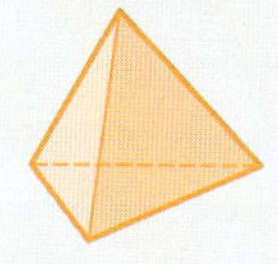

triangular-based pyramid (tetrahedron)

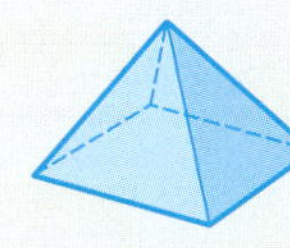

square-based pyramid

William Collins' dream of knowledge for all began with the publication of his first book in 1819.

A self-educated mill worker, he not only enriched millions of lives, but also founded a flourishing publishing house. Today, staying true to this spirit, Collins books are packed with inspiration, innovation and practical expertise.

They place you at the centre of a world of possibility and give you exactly what you need to explore it.

Collins. Freedom to teach.

Published by Collins

An imprint of HarperCollins*Publishers*
The News Building, 1 London Bridge Street, London, SE1 9GF, UK

HarperCollins*Publishers*
Macken House, 39/40 Mayor Street Upper, Dublin 1, D01 C9W8, Ireland

Browse the complete Collins catalogue at
collins.co.uk

10 9 8 7 6 5 4 3 2 1

ISBN 978-0-00-861336-5

British Library Cataloguing-in-Publication Data

A catalogue record for this publication is available from the British Library.

Series editor: Peter Clarke
Cover design and artwork: Amparo Barrera
Internal design concept: Amparo Barrera
Designer: Niki Merrett
Typesetter: David Jimenez
Illustrators: Louise Forshaw, Steven Woods, Gwyneth Williamson and Eva Sassin
Printed and bound in Great Britain by Martins the Printers

MIX
Paper | Supporting responsible forestry
FSC™ C007454

This book is produced from independently certified FSC™ paper to ensure responsible forest management.

For more information visit: harpercollins.co.uk/green

Busy Ant Maths 2nd edition components are compatible with the 1st edition of Busy Ant Maths.